To Natalie with

Best wishes in your yoga journey!

Jesus, Yoga
and
the Way of
Happiness

A Christian Yoga
Daily Devotional

This book is lovingly dedicated to my mother, Marilyn Scott, my husband, Aaron Hebert, and my two sons, Zack and Joshua Hamburg. You are the ones who teach me what it means to love unconditionally every day.

Jesus, Yoga and the Way of Happiness
is written by Andrea J. Vidrine
Copyright 2006, Andrea J. Vidrine

Published and Printed by:
Lifevest Publishing
4901 E. Dry Creek Rd., #170
Centennial, CO 80122
www.lifevestpublishing.com

Printed in the United States of America

I.S.B.N. 1-59879-181-8

Jesus, Yoga

and

the Way of

Happiness

by Andrea J. Vidrine

Table of Contents

Day 1: The Way of Happiness

Psalm 139 Adaptation

Lord, you have searched me and known me.
You know when I sit and when I stand.
You understand my thoughts!
You know when I travel and when I rest.
With all my ways, you are intimately familiar.
Even before a word is on my tongue, Lord, you know it.
Your presence encompasses me. You hold my hand.
Where can I hide from you, Lord?
Where can I run from your love?
If I rise to heaven, you are there.
If I wallow in hell, you are there, too, waiting to lift me up.
If I am overwhelmed by darkness,
the light around me seeming like night,
even the darkness is not dark to you.
The night is as bright as the day.
Darkness and light are but one for you. You will find me.
For you formed my innermost being.
You knit me in my mother's womb.
I praise you, so wonderfully you made me!
Grand are your works!

My very self you knew; my bones were not hidden from you when
I was being made in secret,
fashioned as in the depths of Mother Earth.
Your eyes foresaw all my actions.
The days of my life were written in your book
even before they came to be.
How precious are your designs to me, Oh God, your very
thoughts: the moon and the sun, every grain of sand, every star;
the birds, the fish, and the flowers, each blade of grass;
every hair on every person.
Your creations are infinite and eternal.
Search me, my Lord, and know my heart.
Try me and know my anxious thoughts.
If you see any hurtful way in me,
lead me in your everlasting way.
Teach me to love.

    This book is about happiness and faith. It is my sincere desire that everyone find happiness. Through my studies of the teachings of Jesus and the discipline of yoga, I have found a way of being that results in happiness. And because it works for me, I want to share it with you!

    I believe that God is complete, intimate, unconditional love, and that we are made in His image.[1] God is Love, and we are love. God is Light, and we are light. God loves us more completely than we can possibly imagine. There is nothing that we have done or will ever do that can cause God to love us any less or any more.[2] God loves us because of Who He is and because of who we are. We are His most cherished creation.[3] We are His beloved.[4] He loved us into being, and He has a purpose and a plan for each and every one of us, which includes righteousness, peace, and joy in His Holy Spirit.[5] When we truly understand these concepts on a deep level, we find peace.

Jesus came as Light manifested, Love personified. He came to show us the way. He said, "I am the way, the truth, and the life. No one comes to the Father except by me."[6] He is the anointed One who preaches good news to the poor, announces release to the captives, recovery of sight to the blind, and deliverance to those who are oppressed.[7] He said, "I came so that they may have and enjoy life—and have it in abundance."[8]

What does it mean to come to the Father by Jesus? Jesus said, "I give you a new commandment: Love one another. As I have loved you, so you must love one another. If you have love for one another, then everyone will know that you are my disciples."[9] When we live in a state of loving energy, we experience peace. When we allow bitterness, resentment, and depression to dominate our minds, we suffer. Jesus' message was one of love. When we abide in love, we are following Jesus. He came to show us the way.

Jesus taught that we must repent and be born again in our spirits to experience eternal life.[10] He defined eternal life, not as laying around on a soft, pink, heavenly couch with the television perpetually tuned to your favorite channel; but He said that eternal life is knowledge of God and Himself.[11] Has your idea of repentance been "comply or fry," "turn or burn," "shake or bake?" Repentance actually means to change your mind and leave your old way of being behind. It is a letting go of the small ego-self that dwells on "I, me, mine" and stepping into the God-self, where you know that it is not about you. It's all about God, unselfish love. This self knows that she is made in the image and likeness of God, that God is Light and she is light, that God is Love and she is love. This self knows that the great mystery, as Jesus' disciple, Paul, put it in Colossians 1:27, is that Christ is within you, the hope of glory!

Isaiah 26:3 says, "The Lord will keep in perfect peace him whose mind is stayed on Thee." God speaking through His prophet Isaiah didn't say, "The Lord will keep in perfect peace him whose mind is stayed on *himself*." Matthew 6:33 doesn't read, "Seek first the kingdom of *yourself*, and all things will be added unto you." And Psalm 37:4 doesn't promise, "Seek your happiness in *yourself*, and God will give you your heart's desire." Have you ever noticed that when you keep yourself on your mind you suffer? Jesus said, love, give, lay your life down for your friends. Wash one another's feet. Serve unselfishly. Put yourself last. Put God first. In this knowledge, this eternal life, is the peace which surpasses all understanding.

I invite you to put the principals of which you are about to read into action in your life. There is no physical proof that what Jesus said is true. The proof is in the practice. See if the principles work. Truly put them to the test. Jesus said that a good tree bears good fruit and that his disciples would be known by their fruit. Paul said that the fruit of the Spirit is joy, peace, patience, kindness, goodness, faithfulness, humility, and self-control. If you follow Jesus, you will be amazed at the fruit you produce.

What burden do you carry on your shoulders every day? What do you stress over? Do you worry about how you will pay the bills, succeed at your job, pass your tests in school? Jesus said, "Do not worry. God will provide for you."[12] What would it mean in your life if you actually trusted God to meet all of your needs? If the next time you began to worry about some situation in your life, you simply said, "God supplies all my needs through His riches in Christ Jesus,"[13] and let it go. Well, that is what Jesus is calling us to do. It was not a request when he said, "Do not worry." He meant, "Do not worry!!" This is where radical faith comes in. You must have faith enough to trust God to meet your needs, despite any appearances, sight unseen. You see, we are all walking around with wings on our backs of which we are completely unaware. When we come to the cliff of faith, we look around us and say, "I can't fly." Jesus said, "If you had faith as big as a mustard seed, you could tell this mountain to move from here to there, and it would go."[14] We can't see our wings, but Jesus says that they are there. So all that is left is to take that step. And what you will find when you do, what I have found throughout my life, is that when you trust God to meet all your needs (not just some of them), when you step off of the cliff, you immediately spread your wings and fly.

This book is divided into five main themes that Jesus taught, followed by the discipline of yoga. Once you have an understanding of Jesus' core teachings, I will show you how to use the practices of yoga to facilitate your walk with Christ. I use the Bible (in different translations) as my reference point to the teachings of Jesus and his early followers and the sutras of Patanjali as the basis for the discipline of yoga. Jesus gave us the prescription for a happy and fulfilling life. Once we have the blueprint, however, we must step out on faith and learn to fly.

Question of the Day: What do you value?

Happy Thoughts to Remember

God is love, and whoever lives in love lives in union with God and God lives in union with him . . . There is no fear in love; perfect love drives out all fear.[15]

There is one God and Father of all humankind who is Lord of all, works through all, and is in all.[16]

5

What I teach is not my own teaching, but it comes from God, who sent me. Whoever is willing to do what God wants will know whether what I teach comes from God or whether I speak on my own authority.[17]

1 I John 4:8; Genesis 1:27
2 Romans 8:38-39
3 Matthew 6:26-20
4 John 3:16
5 Jeremiah 29:11; Romans 14:17
6 John 14:6
7 Luke 4:18-21
8 John 10:10, Amplified Bible
9 John 13:34-35
10 Mark 1:14-15; John 3:5
11 John 17:3
12 Matthew 6:33
13 Phillipians 4:19
14 Matthew 17:20
15 I John 4:16,18
16 Ephesians 4:6
17 John 7:17

Day 2: Love One Another

I Corinthians 13:1-8
Amplified Bible

If I speak in the tongues of men and even of angels,
but have not love, I am only a noisy gong or a clanging cymbal.
And if I have prophetic powers and understand all the secret
truths and mysteries and possess all knowledge,
and if I have faith so that I can remove mountains,
but have not love, I am nothing. Even if I dole out all that I have
to the poor, and if I surrender my body to be burned,
but have not love, I gain nothing.
Love endures long and is patient and kind.
Love never is envious nor boils over with jealousy,
is not boastful or vain, does not display itself haughtily.
It is not conceited. It is not rude and does not act unbecomingly.
Love does not insist on its own rights or its own way,
for it is not self-seeking. It is not touchy, fretful, or resentful.
It takes no account of the evil done to it.
It pays no attention to a suffered wrong.
It does not rejoice at injustice and unrighteousness,
but rejoices when right and truth prevail.
Love bears up under anything and everything that comes,

*is ever ready to believe the best of every person, its hopes are
fadeless under all circumstances,
and it endures everything without weakening.
Love never fails.*

It's all about love. I can speak like an angel, give everything I have to the poor, or offer my body on a sacrificial fire, but without love, I am nothing.[18] Jesus taught us that we must love God and one another. He communicated not only with words, but by His example. While he was among us, he healed the sick, raised the dead, and showed compassion to the downtrodden. His command to love was not based on some moral imperative that must be met before we can enter a heavenly realm. Paul said, "For it is by our *faith* that we are put right with God,"[19] and "We know that a person is put right with God only through *faith* in Jesus Christ, never by doing what the Law requires."[20] But rather that the more love we give, the more we will receive. And even further, that we will find lasting happiness and give expression to Christ within us through the path of love. The apostle John said, "Whoever loves his brother lives in the light,"[21] and "Whoever loves is a child of God and knows God."[22] Jesus' entire message is based on this one thing: God loves us, and to experience true happiness we must love Him and each other.

God loves us with an all-encompassing love. We are precious in His sight. Speaking through His prophet, Isaiah, He says, "Do not fear. I have redeemed you. I have called you by name. You are mine. You are precious to me, and I love you.[23] I can never forget you. I have written your name on the palms of my hands.[24] The mountains and hills may crumble, but my love for you will never end.[25] I will show you my love forever."[26] There is nothing in all creation that can ever separate us from God's love.[27]

This is the essence of Love: Love is patient and kind; it is not jealous or conceited or proud; love is not ill-mannered or selfish or irritable; love does not keep a record of wrongs; love is not happy with evil, but is happy with the truth. Love never gives up; and its faith, hope, and patience never fail. Love is eternal.[28]

When I was growing up, I would read these verses and think that surely this was not attainable by a normal person. This stuff was for Mother Theresa, Martin Luther King, Jr., and Gandi. I couldn't be called to never be irritable! You've gotta be kidding. Love's patience never fails?? Right. But as I matured, I realized that the truth of the matter is that this is our calling. Why? Because when we abide in our Christ nature, when we are loving, we are happy. It's that simple. It just doesn't matter what is going on around us. If we are coming from a place of love, we have peace. Come on now, is this just true for me, or have you experienced that when you act with anger, hostility, jealousy, resentment, or out of fear that you lose your peace? It has absolutely consistently proven itself in my life that if I come from a place of fear or anger, etc., that I am not happy. Jesus tells us to love one another because this way, His way, is what will bring us happiness.

Our behavior must not be based on the behavior of other people. Sometimes it seems very difficult to come from a place of unconditional positive regard when the person before us has hurt us in the past, even cruelly and maliciously, hurt someone who is dear to us, or continues to misbehave in the present. It is tempting to allow their actions to be an excuse for us not to answer the high call of love. But we are not called to condone anyone's behavior, or even to like them. We are called, how-ever, to see them as God sees them—as His precious children with a plan and purpose for their lives—and to treat them accordingly. Underneath their earth suit, they are spiritual beings who were created as love and light. Jesus said, "I tell you, whenever you did this for one of the least important of these brothers of mine, you did it for me."[29] When you gaze upon that person who is challenging to love, remember that he is Jesus in disguise.

Paul encouraged, "Eagerly pursue and seek to acquire love, make it your aim, your great quest."[30] Every time you succeed, your heart will smile and your reward will be immediate and self-evident. When you are feeling sad and broken-hearted, find someone to love. You will not have to look far. Call a friend not with the goal of being consoled, but as a consoler. Visit a shut-in. Do yard work or execute a repair for a person in need. Bake cookies and bring them warm and fragrant to the video store clerk, a teacher, the police station, or wherever! Through your reaching out, you will be trading your pity-party for a celebration of love. It works every time. Getting out of yourself and showing compassion for others brings healing. Love begets love.

Be proactive in your love walk. Especially remember the people who inhabit your immediate surroundings. God loves them, too. He wants you to be His hands, His eyes, His voice, and His touch for them to feel His love through you. The people that are in your daily life are God's special gift to you. They are there with the express purpose to love you and to be loved by you. They assist you in your practice of unconditional love. The people who live with you are your first ministry. It is important that you target them as your primary love projects. How can you serve them today? How can you let them know that you love them and that God loves them? In this service, you will find happiness.

<u>Question of the Day:</u> Who needs to hear, "I love you," from you today?

<u>Happy Thoughts to Remember</u>

My commandment is this: love one another just as I love you. The greatest love a person can have for his friends is to give his life for them.[31]

Love one another. As I have loved you, so you must love one another. If you have love for one another, then everyone will know that you are my disciples.[32]

Let us love one another, because love comes from God. Whoever loves is a child of God and knows God. Whoever does not love does not know God, for God *is* love.[33]

---

18 I Corinthians 13
19 Romans 10:10
20 Galatians 2:16
21 I John 2:10
22 I John 4:7
23 Isaiah 43:1, 5
24 Isaiah 49:16
25 Isaiah 54:10
26 Isaiah 49:8
27 Romans 8:39
28 I Corinthians 13:4-8
29 Matthew 25:40
30 I Corinthians 14:1, Amplified Bible
31 John 15:13
32 John 13:34
33 I John 4:7-8

Day 3: Have Faith in God.
You Can Do Anything!

Psalm 27 Adaptation

The Lord is my Light and my Salvation. Whom shall I fear?
The Lord is the Refuge of my life. Of whom shall I be afraid?
When the wicked, even my enemies, came upon me to devour me,
they stumbled and fell. Though a host encamp against me,
my heart shall not fear. Though war arise against me,
even in this will I be confident.
One thing have I asked of the Lord, this will I seek,
that I may dwell in His Presence all the days of my life,
to behold His beauty and gaze upon His delightful loveliness,
to meditate in the temple of His love. For in the day of trouble,
He will hide me in His shelter.
In His secret place will He hide me.
He will set me high upon a rock,
above the canyon and the valley, where I can even see the sea.
And now shall my head be lifted up above my troubles
all around me. I will shout for joy and sing,
yes sing praises to the Lord!
Hear, Oh Lord, when I cry aloud.
Have mercy and be gracious to me and answer me!
You have said, "Seek My face," and my heart cries out to you,

"I will seek Your face! Hide not your face from me,
Oh God of my salvation!"
Although my father and my mother forsake me,
yet the Lord will take me up. Teach me Your way,
O Lord, and lead me in a plain and even path.
Give me not up to the will of my flesh,
for false imaginings have risen up against me.
They breathe out cruelty and violence.
They tempt me from Your Love. What would have become of me
had I not believed in the splendor of Your Presence!
Wait, hope for, and expect the Lord.
Be brave and of good courage.
Let your heart be stout and enduring.
Yes, wait for, hope for, and expect the Lord!

As we abide in the nature of Jesus and let his words dominate our minds, we receive the answers to our prayers.[34] Jesus taught that we have all the power of God available to us as His children. He brought the message that God loves us as His cherished own, and therefore He will provide for us in every way. You know that as a parent, you would want your child to have complete provision. How much more does the One who loves us so completely want to see our needs fulfilled? If we will just have faith in our Father, we can do anything.

Jesus gave four practical teachings on authority set in a background of reverence and humility:

1. When we put God first, all things are provided for us.
2. If we ask, we will receive.
3. If we ask for anything in His name, He will do it.
4. When we pray, we speak the answer, believe we have received, and forgive any offenses.

When Jesus performed miracles, he spoke and it came to pass. He ordered the winds and the waves to be calm, and they quieted.[35] He told a paralyzed man to pick up his mat and go home and he did.[36] With a word, he raised a little girl from death to life.[37] It is by our faith-filled words that we live in victory or defeat. Jesus said that his followers must imitate him in every way. We must serve each other and do the works that he did and even further them. Paul said, "Since you are God's dear children, you must try to be like him."[38]

Death and life are in the power of the tongue.[39] Jesus was very clear on this point. He said, "Have faith in God. I assure you that whoever tells this hill to get up and throw itself in the sea and does not doubt in his heart, but believes that what he says will happen, it will be done for him. For this reason I tell you, when you pray and ask for something, believe that you have received it, and you will be given whatever you ask for. And when you stand and pray, forgive anything you may have against anyone, so that your Father in heaven will forgive the wrongs you have done."[40] The power of God is available to each and every one of us. The question is, do we have the faith to wield it? Jesus said that all things are possible to him who believes.[41] He didn't say that *some* things are possible. And he didn't say that when you stand praying, believe that you have received and it *might* come to pass. What he did say is that if you speak to the mountain and do not doubt, it *will* move. Everyone who asks, receives.[42] We walk by faith and not by sight.[43]

Paul illustrates the power of faith when he talks about the heroes of old who trusted God and exercised their authority as His children, therefore conquering adversity. "Through faith they fought whole countries and won. They did what was right and received what God had promised. They shut the mouths of lions, put out fierce fires, escaped being killed by the sword. They were weak, but became strong; they were mighty in battle and defeated the armies of foreigners. Through faith, women received their dead relatives back to life."[44]

14

These things that they did were accomplished through faith in God.

What mountains do you need to speak to in your life? What trees must be uprooted? I believe that in many cases, people hear and understand Jesus' message of love, repentance, and forgiveness, but fail to recognize his teaching on power. We have all the power that Jesus demonstrated at our disposal. It is simply up to us to claim it by faith. This means that we must follow the example that Jesus set and imitate our Father "whose command brings into being what did not exist."[45]

So in a practical sense, how do you begin demonstrating your faith and walking in power? First you search your heart for any un-forgiveness and let it go. Then you ask, believe, and speak.[46] You must speak not the problem, but the answer, thanking God daily for the victory.[47] Jesus gave us a wonderful example of how to assert our authority and to conquer adversity. When the devil tempted him in the wilderness, Jesus responded by saying, "It is written . . ."[48] He used holy scripture as a sword to cut through the darkness. If you follow his example, you must familiarize yourself with the verses that address the challenge you are facing and speak these positive statements out loud with thanksgiving. Do not let one negative word depart from your lips. "Stop judging by mere appearances, but make a right judgment."[49] Instead, build yourself up with the Word of God. Do not be moved by what you feel or what you see. As Paul says, "Therefore put on the full armor of God, so that when the day of evil comes, you may be able to stand your ground, and after you have done everything, **to stand**."[50]

The bible is not a book of spells and incantations, however. Making positive statements should not be thought of as a formula for success. Rather, we speak to build our confidence and to demonstrate our faith in God. Faith without demonstration is merely thought. Speaking out what we believe we have received is staking our claim with positive expectation.

Let all your words be filled with praise and gratitude. Affirm and thank God for your health while you are healthy. Praise God for your riches when the money is already there. And stand firm, never doubting, when you are calling those things "into being that did not exist." Believe in the power of God in your life, and you will be amazed at the results.

"But having faith in the midst of adversity," you say, "is not easy. When all around me exists a mountain of evidence that seems too real to move, I just can't believe. If I don't know how it can possibly work out, how *can* I believe? I feel like a fool!" If you knew the blessings on the other side of the mountain, you would get busy moving it! The thing is, the choice is yours: fear or faith. If you have peace living in doubt and fear, then by all means, keep on trucking. But if by chance, you seek the peace **beyond understanding**, then choose faith. Choose faith.

I have gone so far in my life to avoid having to prove my faith, that I have denied the existence of problems. "Maybe they will just go away on their own. Then I won't have to risk trusting God only to be disappointed." Have you ever played that mind game? It's not a happy place. You know the "Doubting Thomas" mindset, "What if I fail? I know my faith is not strong enough." Yes, but what if you succeed! Really the only part that is about you at all, is that you must be willing to ask. God does the rest. The defining moment came for me when I realized that the power of God is revealed to the unbelieving world when one of us steps out in faith. Yes, I know, kind of obvious, but it wasn't to me.

So now, I want to choose faith because it is only then that I can glorify God when beyond all my imaginings, a miracle occurs. If I do not step out, how can I brag about my beautiful Lord? With what proof do I have to show His glory to the world? Jesus said, "I will do whatever you ask for in my name, so that the Father's glory will be shown through the Son."[51] I want to be a vehicle for the glory of God. And the amazing part is, I just have to ask.

Question of the Day: What is one belief that you hold that is limiting you?

Happy Thoughts to Remember

All things are possible to him who believes![52]

All things are possible with God.[53]

Do not, therefore, fling away your fearless confidence, for it carries a great and glorious compensation of reward. For you have need of steadfast patience and endurance, so that you may perform and fully accomplish the will of God, and thus receive and carry away what is promised.[54]

---

34 John 15:7
35 Matthew 7:8-11
36 Matthew 8:26
37 Matthew 9:6
38 Mark 5:41
39 Ephesians 5:1-2
40 Proverbs 18:21
41 Mark 11:22-24
42 Mark 9:23
43 Matthew 7:8
44 II Corinthians 5:7
45 Hebrews 11:33-35
46 Romans 4:17
47 II Corinthians 4:13
48 See, for instance, the bible affirmations in the appendix.
49 Matthew 4:1-11
50 John 7:24
51 Ephesians 6:13
52 John 14:13
53 Mark 9:23
54 Matthew 19:26
55 Hebrews 10:35-36

Day 4: As You Sow, So You Reap

Psalm 37 & Psalm 118, Selected Verses

Trust in the Lord and do good;
so shall you dwell in the land and feed surely
on His faithfulness, and truly you shall be fed!
Delight yourself in the Lord
and He will give you the desires of your heart.
Commit your way to the Lord; trust in Him and He will do this:
He will make your righteousness shine like the dawn,
the justice of your cause like the noonday sun.
Be still before the Lord and wait patiently for him.
Give thanks to the Lord, for He is good.
His love endures forever. Let Israel say,
"His love endures forever!" Let the house of Aaron say,
"His love endures forever!" I will not die but live,
and will proclaim what the Lord has done.
This is the day the Lord has made.
Let us rejoice and be glad in it! You are my God,
and I will give you thanks. You are my God,
and I will exalt you! Give thanks to the Lord,
for He is good. His love endures forever.

My mother is a very generous person. Just ask anyone, they'll tell you. She sends just about everyone she knows a birthday card—every year; and she knows a lot of people! When a family member is in financial trouble, she sends money—every month. When a family friend dies, she gives food and comfort. She calls friends that she knows need her attention. She spoils me and my family rotten. She looks for opportunities to help. She is a giver. And as anyone who understands spiritual law might expect, she is known as "a woman who has everything." Do you know anyone like that? Actually, I hope it's you! If it isn't right now, it can be. The giving train is rolling into the station. Climb aboard.

Jesus taught that what we give out, we get back.[56] This is a very important message to grasp. When we truly understand the concept, we will want to do as much as we can, in every way we can, for as many people as we can! The amount that we want to be prospered and in the variety of ways, is the measure we must use to prosper other people. Do you hoard your wealth? Do you choose to share? When you see someone in need, do you pass them by? What is your attitude toward other people? Do you look for opportunities to serve? The more we give of ourselves and our resources, the more we are blessed.

We are like channels for the waters of life. When the channel is clear, the flow of prosperity is unimpeded. We bless others and are in turn blessed. A smooth, abundant flow rushes through us continually. This relates not only to our giving of financial resources and time, but also to the thoughts we think and the words we speak about others. When our channel is not gummed up with negative attitudes and speech, the waters of life flow peacefully through. When we damn our channels with judgment, bitterness, and condemnation, we create a whirlpool of discontent within our souls.

When you feel emotional discomfort, this is your clue that the flow of water through your channel is being impeded. This is the time to go into meditation and notice what thoughts come your way. Are you replaying a recent conversation over and over trying to change the outcome? Are you feeling angry, blaming someone else for a condition in your life? Are you beating yourself up for some sin you think is unforgivable? Once you become aware of the cause of your discontent, it is time to clean the channel out. Dwelling on a challenge or uncomfortable emotion will not open your channel. You must take loving action.

Be pro-active. Pray for the wisdom to know the direction you should take and the grace to be non-violent in your thoughts, speech, and actions. Then address the issue as best you can, surrendering the outcome to God. Jesus said, "If you are about to offer your gift to God at the altar and there you remember that your brother has something against you, leave your gift there in front of the altar, go at once and make peace with your brother, and then come back and offer your gift to God."[57] Do what needs to be done now, then know that the best that you can do is to act with pure intentions. The result of your actions is beyond your control. You cannot orchestrate how someone will receive your endeavors or how they will react. Offering your sincere efforts to God is the highest ideal and the one that will bring peace.

Once you have taken appropriate action, the next step is to keep the channel of your mind cleared out of thought clutter. Release the "what ifs," the "how might I haves," and the "I'm not worthy's." As you think, so you are[58] and as you sow, so you reap.[59] What do you want to be? If you want to be peaceful, you must think peaceful thoughts. If you want to be pure, you must think pure thoughts. If you want to be happy, you must think happy thoughts. Daily plant affirmative ideas that suffuse your mind with positive expectations.[60] Say them out loud. Sing them to yourself. Whatever things are true, honest, just, pure, lovely, and of good report, having virtue and being praiseworthy, think on these things.[61]

Jesus said, "Give and it will be given to you, good measure, pressed down, shaken together, all that you can hold; the measure you use for others is the measure that will be used for you."[62] Wow, that's a daunting thought! The measure I use for others is the one that will be used for me. If I want abundant happiness, then I must bring happiness to others in the measure that I want to receive it. If I want peace, I must be the presence of peace in my interactions with others. If I want love, then I must be a loving person. If I want financial increase, then I must give of my monetary resources. If I want a healthy body, I must sow exercise and conscious eating. Our lives are fields ready to be planted with the seeds of our hearts' desires.

When we get ready to plant a garden, we buy a little seed bag that shows exactly what we want to grow. This, too, is the first step in living our dreams. We must have a clear picture of where we want to go or what we want to grow. Then we prepare the soil to receive a seed. In the garden of our lives, this means that we need to do a searching moral inventory which reveals any roots of bitterness, resentment, condescension, arrogance, and un-forgiveness. We prepare the soil by repenting and making amends.[63] Then we plant the seeds that produce the harvest that we desire. We cannot plant spinach and expect to get daffodils. And if we plant nothing at all, that is exactly what we get. As we sow, so shall we reap. We must sow to reap a harvest.

In turn, we must nurture the dream by pulling out the weeds that can choke out our growth along the way. Jesus said, "If your right eye serves as a trap to ensnare you or is an occasion for you to stumble and sin, pluck it out and throw it away. It is better that you lose one of your members than that your whole body be cast into hell."[64] And Paul affirmed, "Leave no room or foothold for the devil (give no opportunity to him)."[65] Weeds in our gardens give the devil an opportunity to steal our peace. Every negative thought and word, every subtle temptation, every obstacle to happiness, must be uprooted and discarded. If your weed is alcohol, don't hang out at the bar. If lust grows easily in your heart, don't have lunch with that sexy co-worker. Pull out the weeds before they choke your dreams.

Your life right now is the garden that you planted yesterday. If you don't like your harvest, then uproot and replant. All it takes is a change of mind. New thoughts + new words + new actions = new results.

Get a picture of your heart's desire. Hold it always in the forefront of your mind, and thank God constantly that it is done. Keep the field of your mind well-tended and planted with good seed. Get on the giving train. Its destination is all the love, forgiveness, peace, and happiness that you can hold!

Question of the Day: What weeds need to be pulled out of the garden of your life?

Happy Thoughts to Remember

He who sows generously will also reap generously and with blessings.[66]

Give and it will be given to you—good measure, pressed down, shaken together and running over, will be poured into your lap.[67]

Whatever a man sows, this he will also reap.[68]

---

56 Luke 6:38
57 Matthew 5:23-24
58 Proverbs 23:7
59 Galatians 6:7
60 See, for instance, the bible affirmations in the appendix.
61 Phillipians 4:6-8
62 Luke 6:38
63 Hebrews 12:15
64 Matthew 5:29
65 Ephesians 4:27
66 II Corinthians 9:6
67 Luke 6:38
68 Galatians 6:7

Day 5: Make the Most of What You Have Been Given

I Hope You Dance
by Mark D. Sanders & Tia Sillers

I hope you never lose your sense of wonder.
You get your fill to eat, but always keep that hunger.
May you never take one single breath for granted.
God forbid love ever leave you empty handed.
I hope you still feel small when you stand beside the ocean.
Whenever one door closes I hope one more opens.
Promise me that you'll give faith a fighting chance.
And when you get the choice to sit it out or dance,
I hope you dance. I hope you never fear
those mountains in the distance;
Never settle for the path of least resistance.
Living might mean taking chances, but they're worth taking.
Loving might be a mistake, but it's worth making.
Don't let some hell-bent heart leave you bitter.
When you come close to selling out, reconsider.
Give the heavens above more than just a passing glance.
And when you get the choice to sit it out or dance,
I hope you dance.
Time is a wheel in constant motion always rolling us along.

*Tell me who wants to look back
on their years and wonder where those years have gone.
I hope you dance.*

The lights are on and people are visiting their way in. I am standing on stage in eager anticipation. The harmony that revealed itself to me only tentatively during practice, flows forth with an intensity that I know comes only from Christ within. My small ego-sense-of-self could not produce that sound. In the music that is issuing forth from my body is a sense of timelessness. I am the Light. We are One, and I know it. Do you know what I mean?

I am whirling around the dance floor. I am free in my partner's hands. The momentum is exhilarating, and I am one with the rhythm. The joy of movement overwhelms me. There is no thought. Do you remember a feeling like that?

I am teaching and I feel a presence speaking through me that I recognize as Christ. It cannot be any other way, for from where did the insight come? It is not of my small self. I am in the zone. Do you recognize that space?

Jesus told a story about a rich man who was about to embark on a journey.[69] He gathered his servants together and gave one five talents (money), another two talents, and the last, one talent. He did this according to the ability of each servant. When the man returned, the one with five talents had earned five more, the one with two talents, two more, but the servant with one talent had buried his in the ground. The man commended the first two servants heartily with, "Well done, you good and faithful servant," sharing his joy with them and giving them even more to work with.

What have you done with the talents that God has given you? You have this one life, even this one day. What will you make of it to the glory of God? Do you know that when you are doing the things that you do well, that spark your curiosity, that bring you the most joy, that you are serving God to the fullest by honoring the talents that He has blessed you with? We all have talents and interests. Jesus taught that we must make the most of what we have been given.

If you don't know where your talent lies, then try new things. Some people know right away what their gifts are. Others have to go through a process of trial and error to discover where they excel. Talents come in all different shapes and sizes. They do not have to be complex to be worthy of expression. Simple gifts are just as lovely as intricate abilities. Paul uses the analogy of a body with its many components.[70] All the parts are needed for the synergistic expression of the organism. Without our eyes, we cannot see. Without our feet, we cannot walk. The many members form a beautiful whole. And so it is with the family of humanity, each one expressing the glory of God in his own special way. Find that activity that makes your face light up and your body vibrate with energy. This is your arena in which to shine.

Everything on earth exists to serve. We were not created for ourselves, but to be a part of a greater good, each making a contribution to the sustenance of the collective. A candle was created to burn and give light. Trees cleanse our air by taking in carbon dioxide and releasing oxygen. Earthworms renew our soil. Tomato plants bear fruit that we eat. You were given your talents to enrich the larger whole. The beauty in the plan is that your area of service was also designed to give you the greatest joy. As you give, you also receive. You are part of a dynamic system that exists to serve.

We have just one life to live. This means that our opportunity to feel the exhilaration of doing those things that bring us joy lasts only for the duration of that life, however short or long it may be. What a shame if we let this precious opportunity pass us by! While we are on earth, we are God's hands, God's eyes, God's mouth. Through us, God manifests a myriad of talents and good works. If you are not already expressing your talents in ways that are satisfying for you, don't delay!

You may be gone from this earth tomorrow. Realize your dream. Practice your talents. Pursue your interests. Shine your light for all to see. In this way, God is glorified through you, the world is blessed by your contribution, and you are filled with satisfaction. What an awesome feeling to know that you are living your one life to its fullest!

Question of the Day: What are two of your talents?

Happy Thoughts to Remember

Well done, good and faithful servant! You have been faithful with a few things; I will put you in charge of many things. Come and share your master's happiness![71]

The one who received the seed that fell on good soil is the man who hears the Word and understands it. He produces a crop, yielding a hundred, sixty, or thirty times what was sown.[72]

You are the light of the world. A city set on a hill cannot be hidden. Nor do men light a lamp and put it under a peck measure, but on a lampstand, and it gives light to all in the house. Let your light so shine before men that they may see your good deeds and recognize and praise your Father Who is in heaven.[73]

---

69 Matthew 25:14-30
70 I Corinthians 12
71 Matthew 25:21
72 Matthew 13:23
73 Matthew 5:14-16

Day 6: Forgive

Pray don't find fault with the man who limps
Or stumbles along the road,
Unless you have worn the shoes he wears
Or struggled beneath his load.
There may be tacks in his shoes that hurt,
Though hidden away from view,
Or the burden he bears, placed on your back,
Might cause you to stumble, too.
Don't sneer at the man who's down today,
unless you have felt the blow
That caused his fall, or felt the same that only the fallen know.
You may be strong,
But still the blows that were his, if dealt to you
In the self-same way at the self-same time,
Might cause you to stagger, too.
Don't be too harsh with the man who sins,
Or pelt him with words or stones,
Unless you are sure, yea, doubly sure,
That you have no sins of your own.
For you know, perhaps if the tempter's voice

Should whisper as soft to you
As it did to him when he went astray,
'twould cause you to falter, too.

The times when I find it hardest to forgive are the times when my ego is involved. You know the way it goes. Someone said or did something that "made" you look bad. Well, anyway, that's how it goes for me. I don't want to look bad. I don't like to be seen as less than competent, nice, and considerate. But the truth is that what other people say and do is a reflection of them, not of you (or me)! If someone criticizes me, it is a reflection of their character. If someone yells at me or hurts my feelings or in other ways betrays me, it shows their ego dramas. I really don't have to get involved in their play. I can choose to simply watch and forgive them for not being perfect. After all, I'm not perfect either. I have my own dramas. I have made, and have the potential to continue to make, poor choices. So does everyone else. To the extent that I can remove myself from their productions is the extent to which I will experience peace.

True happiness cannot be experienced if we are living in a state of un-forgiveness. Jesus taught that in all things we must forgive those who wrong us. He said, "If your brother sins, rebuke him, and if he repents, forgive him. If he sins against you seven times in one day, and each time he comes to you saying, 'I repent,' you must forgive him."[74] He powerfully stated, "Let he who is without sin cast the first stone."[75] You may look at your offender and think that you would *never* do what he did. But there is something else that you *would* do. We will not experience peace with a "holier than thou" attitude. We all have sinned and fallen short of the glory of God.[76] When we harbor resentment and bitterness, we are eaten away from the inside out. The flow of blessings, our healing, and the joyful expression of our talents are all inhibited by our un-forgiveness. You cannot experience God's abundant blessings and healing if you are unforgiving. You hurt yourself more than anyone else when you hang on to your crown of martyrdom.

Forgiving others is essential if we want to experience peace in our lives, and likewise we must release ourselves from our own condemnation. Do thoughts of unworthiness cloud your mind when you have missed the mark and hurt your brother or sister? When I am the cause of another's pain, I just want to crawl in a hole and die. I feel so unworthy to even breathe. But when we confess our sin to God, He is faithful and just to forgive us of all unrighteousness.[77] He remembers our sins no more. If God releases you from condemnation, even forgetting your transgressions, then let yourself off of the hook.[78] You are no good to yourself or anyone else when you are walking around in a state of self-judgment. That is a very self-centered place to be. Accept God's forgiveness, commit yourself to repentance (a change of your mind), and move forward with the joy of expressing God in all you are. Take the bag off of your head. You are His light.

So in restoring the flow of favor in your life the answer is always the same. You must forgive the ones who have harmed you, and you must forgive yourself. Release them to their highest good. If the opportunity exists to express your pain to them in a non-violent way, you must do it. Remember Jesus' instruction to make peace with our brothers before we approach the altar of God?[79] This gives them the chance to repent and to ask for your forgiveness. If there is no means by which you may speak to the ones who have hurt you, then you must forgive and release them by the grace of God, knowing that in most cases, they were acting from their own pain and perceived hurt. "Hurting" people hurt people. If we could see our brothers and sisters from the viewpoint of God, we would forgive them instantly and effortlessly, knowing all the circumstances that led to their actions. We would know their pain.

Whether you believe it or not, just like you, they were doing the best they could with the knowledge they had. Don't you want that kind of acceptance? Jesus put it this way, "Father, forgive them. They do not know what they are doing."[80]

Question of the Day: Who do you need to forgive today?

Happy Thoughts to Remember

Forgive others and God will forgive you.[81]

I, even I, am He Who blots out and cancels your transgressions for My own sake, and remembers your sins no more.[82]

As far as the east is from the west, so far has He removed our transgressions from us.[83]

74 Luke 17:3-4
75 John 8:7
76 Romans 3:23
77 I John 1:9
78 Isaiah 43:25
79 Matthew 5:23-24
80 Luke 23:34
81 Luke 6:37
82 Isaiah 43:25
83 Psalm 103:12

Day 7: Yoga

A Poem by Rumi

I am dust particles in sunlight.
I am the round sun.
To the bits of dust I say, Stay; To the sun, Keep moving.
I am morning mist and the breathing of evening.
I am wind in the top of a grove, and surf of the cliff.
Mast, rudder, helmsman, and keel,
I am also the coral reef they flounder on.
I am a tree with a trained parrot in its branches.
Silence, thought, and voice.
The musical air coming through a flute, a spark off a stone,
a flickering in metal.
Both candle and the moth crazy around it.
Rose and the nightingale lost in the fragrance.
I am all orders of being, the circling galaxy,
the evolutionary intelligence,
the lift and the falling away.
What is and what isn't.
You who know Jelaluddin,
you the One in all, say who I am.

The meaning of the word *yoga* is to yoke up or to join; union. Yoga is walking in the awareness of your union with Christ. It is abiding in the nature of Christ in every moment; being the presence of Love. The tenets of yoga were written down by a sage named Patanjali in a manual called the yoga sutras. Sutra means thread. The book that Patanjali wrote is a compilation of oral tradition that was written as brief threads of wisdom with very little embellishment. The sutras were intended as a guide to be used in conjunction with instruction from a master teacher.

In the yoga sutras, Patanjali defines the discipline of yoga as the restraint of the modifications of the mind.[84] Put in simple terms, yoga is the control of the wanderings of the mind. The mind is often likened to a drunken monkey swinging here and there, a thing out of control. When the mind is untrained, much of our time is spent planning for the future, dwelling on the past, obsessing about mistakes, blaming, judging, complaining, etc., etc., etc. This type of thinking does not bring peace and joy to our lives, but rather keeps us bound into states of defeat. Whatever thoughts that we hold in mind the most will create the reality of our lives. It is not the things that happen on the outside that construct our reality, it is what we *think* about those things that forms our world. Proverbs 4:23 says, "Be careful how you think. Your life is shaped by your thoughts." If your mind is a place of judgment and disorder, then chances are that your life will seem critical and chaotic to you. If your mind is a place of harmony and love, then no matter what circumstance you are confronted with, you experience peace.

Our lives are comprised of a series of events and our reactions. First something happens. Then we have a thought about it. Next we feel an emotion related to the thought. Finally, we choose our reaction.

EVENT—THOUGHT—EMOTION—REACTION

32

Without training the mind to become aware of thoughts, part of this process occurs unconsciously. We are aware of the event, our emotions, and our reaction, but we are often clueless as to the thought that directed our course of action.

Let's take a simple illustration for example. You see Mary walking by and you greet her with an enthusiastic "hello." Mary doesn't respond and keeps on walking (event). You think (probably unconsciously), "Wow, what a rude person!" (thought). Your heart rate accelerates, and your face feels flushed. You recognize feeling embarrassed and somewhat angry (emotion). Next time you see Mary, you intentionally turn your head and pass her by (reaction). This choice may have given you momentary satisfaction, but it did little to produce positive feelings or to create peace in your life.

So from this basic illustration, it is evident that there were many choices in what to think and how to react. Suppose you chose to think, "Oh, Mary probably didn't hear me," or "Mary must be lost in thought," or any other conciliatory thought. Then you might choose to greet Mary enthusiastically again the next time you see her. This choice would create harmony in your mind, rather than discord.

Emotions are our barometer. They indicate the status of our thought life. Feelings are not good or bad, but rather road signs on the journey. Angry, sad, selfish feelings, indicate fleshly thoughts.[85] The sign says, "Choose other thoughts." But if you are attached to your ego dramas, you always have the choice to continue the experience. Happy, joyful, peaceful feelings suggest that your thoughts are aligned with Spirit.[86] The sign reads, "Keep on thinking."

Emotions can be powerful forces in our lives, especially in relation to our loved ones. People who are closest to us in the world have the greatest power to hurt us because we care most about them. We give them this power. The most painful events involving

33

our loved ones in our daily lives tend to have a more complex effect. We interact with someone and then feel angry, sad, hurt, or whatever emotion and usually aren't aware of the thought behind the feeling. This is when the practice of yoga is the most beneficial. A strong negative emotion is the indicator that we are having a disturbing thought. The practice is to take the time to discover what the thought is. Once we become aware of what we are thinking in relation to the event, we can decide if we agree with the thought. It may take some clarification. At that point, perhaps we would check in with the offending person and say something like, "I'm thinking 'thus and so.' Is that what you meant? Is that correct?" We cannot choose our feelings, but we can choose our thoughts; but first we have to be aware of them. Real life transformation begins on the thought level. Paul reminded us that love believes the best of every person and that we must keep our minds set on the higher things.[87] God transforms us inwardly by a change of mind.[88]

Paul said, "The weapons of our warfare are not physical, but they are mighty before God for the overthrow and destruction of strongholds."[89] The strongholds are not the events that happen in our lives, but our thoughts about the events. The battle is in the mind. He goes on to say, "We refute arguments and every proud thing that sets itself up against the true knowledge of God; and we lead every thought away captive into the obedience of Christ."[90] God is love, therefore every thought that is not loving is a "proud thing set up against the true knowledge of God." John said, "He who dwells in love dwells in God and God dwells and continues in him."[91]

The most important thing that you can do to create peace in your life is to keep your mind focused on Christ, the Light of the world Who lives in you, the hope of glory.[92] You are not your thoughts or your desires and preferences. It is when you identify with the endless stream of mind chatter and peculiarities which you

34

call your "self" (your ego), that suffering results. Yoga in its purest form is the experience of Christ within you, unconditional Love, total surrender. When we abide in this Christ-awareness, we feel serene. God promises to keep us in perfect peace when we keep our minds fixed on Him.[93] By consciously making the effort to quiet the mind, stop the train of thoughts, and then choosing to yield to Christ, we experience yoga.

Question of the Day: What do you spend most of your time thinking about?

Happy Thoughts to Remember

The Kingdom of God is within you.[94]

Be still and know that I Am God.[95]

The Lord will keep in perfect peace Him whose mind is stayed on Thee.[96]

---

84 Sutra 1:2
85 Galatians 5: 19-21
86 Galatians 5: 22-23
87 I Corinthians 13:7, Colossians 3:2
88 Romans 12:2
89 II Corinthians 10:4
90 II Corinthians 10:5
91 I John 4:16
92 Colossians 1:27
93 Isaiah 26:3
94 Luke 17:21
95 Psalm 46:10
96 Isaiah 26:3

Day 8: Effort Toward Steadiness of Mind

Two Poems by Rumi

Come, come, come!
Come, whoever you are! Wanderer, worshipper,
lover of leaving.
This is not a caravan of despair.
It doesn't matter if you've broken your vow
a thousand times,
still and yet again come!

Out beyond ideas of wrong-doing
& right-doing
there is a field.
I'll meet you there.

Wouldn't a break from endless thinking be a delicious treat? I know. I feel the same way. There is peace in the silence, that delightful space between thoughts. In the Christian yoga classes that I teach, we use many techniques to quiet the mind. We chant, breathe consciously, pay attention to the sensations in our body, experience the space around us, and meditate. It is a yummy experience and one that you can create at home by using the practices that work best for you. Once you begin, you're hooked.

It is true, the key to victorious living is in the training of the mind. Patanjali said that the mind is trained in two ways: through practice and non-attachment.[97] Practice involves four things: effort toward steadiness of mind,[98] tapas (discipline), study, and surrendering to God.[99] Non-attachment refers to offering the actions of our lives to God without trying to manipulate the outcomes, and looking to God as our source of peace and not to other people, objects, activities, food, or substances.

The first form of practice is effort toward steadiness of mind. Anything that you do to steady your mind is considered to be practice. The discipline of yoga offers specific tools to train the mind. Here are some of the techniques:

1. "To repeat the name of God with reflection on its meaning is an aid."[100] Proverbs 18:10 says, "The name of the Lord is a strong tower; the righteous run into it and are safe," and Paul admonishes us to "keep our eyes fixed on Jesus on whom our faith depends from beginning to end."[101] The silent repetition of the name of God or of a sacred word or phrase is called japa. The sacred word or phrase is called your mantra. Mantra repetition takes your mind off of any worries, fear, dread, or negative thinking. The highest mantra in the Christian tradition is the name of Jesus. However, a favorite Bible verse, a meaningful phrase (Come Lord Jesus, God is love, Abba Father, God is with me, etc.), a verse from a song, other names of God, or any inspirational phrase of your choice can be used.

   Japa is a continual practice that may be performed at any time during the day or night. It is especially useful, though, to set aside a regular time for meditation, when you only practice silent mantra repetition. Thoughts will come and go during this time. The discipline is to continue to bring your focus back to your mantra. Repeating the name of Jesus silently is the most important practice. "From this practice, all obstacles disappear and knowledge of the true Self emerges."[102]

2. "Calm is retained by breath control."[103] "It is the Spirit of God that made me, and the breath of the Almighty that gives me life."[104] God breathes in us. Paying conscious attention to the breath is called pranayama. Pranayama is literally the control of prana or energy. When the breath becomes conscious, the mind becomes quiet. Here is a simple breathing practice: Let the air flow in and out through your nostrils, rather than your mouth. Inhale deep into your belly drawing the breath up through your rib cage, expanding it front to back and side to side, and then to your upper chest. Pause to retain your breath a moment. Exhale first from the belly, then the rib cage, and then the upper chest. Slow the breath way down and allow your mind to become quiet. When thoughts come into your head, let them go and bring your attention back to your breath. This breathing practice can be done at any time, but is especially effective lying on your back with your eyes closed. "Let everything that has breath and every breath of life praise the Lord!"[105]

3. "Concentrating on the supreme, ever-blissful Light within"[106] opens awareness of your union with Christ. "The Lord shall be to you an everlasting light,"[107] "the true Light coming into the world that illumines every person."[108] This simple practice is to dwell on the warm

and blissful Light of Christ within you. Let your thoughts float by like clouds in a clear blue sky. "In Him was Life, and the Life was the Light of men. And the Light shines on in the darkness, for the darkness has never overpowered it."[109]

4. "By cultivating attitudes of friendliness toward the happy, compassion for the unhappy, delight in the virtuous, and disregard toward the wicked, the mind remains calm."[110] Cultivate a cheerful attitude with yourself and everyone you meet. This trains your mind by consciously choosing to be a bearer of joy in the world in every situation. "Clothe yourselves therefore, as God's own chosen ones who are purified, holy, and well-beloved by God Himself, by putting on behavior marked by tenderhearted pity and mercy, kind feeling, a lowly opinion of yourselves, gentle ways, and patience."[111]

Training the mind absolutely works and will bring you amazing results toward peace of mind. My friend, Julie, has a unique way to take her thoughts captive when faced with potential offense. She says, "This is (person's name) that the Lord has made. I will rejoice and be glad in him." In this way, she immediately brings her focus to the way God views the person. This is the technique that works for her. Find the one that brings you success. As you think, so you are.[112]

Question of the Day: What effort toward steadiness of mind are you willing to commit to today?

Happy Thoughts to Remember

A calm and undisturbed mind and heart are the life and health of the body.[113]

Let us fix our eyes on Jesus, the author and perfecter of our faith, who for the joy set before him endured the cross, scorning its shame, and sat down at the right hand of the throne of God.[114]

Whatever is true, whatever is noble, whatever is right, whatever is pure, whatever is lovely, whatever is admirable—if anything is excellent or praiseworthy—think on these things.[115]

---

97 Sutra 1:12
98 Sutra 1:13
99 Sutra 2:1
100 Sutra 1:28
101 Hebrews 12:2
102 Sutra 1:29
103 Sutra 1:34
104 Job 33:4
105 Psalm 150:6
106 Sutra 1:36
107 Isaiah 60:19
108 John 1:9
109 John 1:4-5
110 Sutra 1:33
111 Colossians 3:12
112 Proverbs 23:7
113 Proverbs 14:30
114 Hebrews 12:2
115 Philippians 4:8

Day 9: Tapas

Learning Christ
(unknown author)

Teach me, my Lord, to be sweet and gentle
in all the events of life—
In disappointments,
In the thoughtlessness of others,
In the insincerity of those I trusted,
In the unfaithfulness of those on whom I relied.
Let me put myself aside to think of the happiness of others,
To hide my little pains and heartaches,
So that I may be the only one to suffer from them.
Teach me to profit by the suffering that comes across my path.
Let me so use it that it may mellow me,
not harden nor embitter me;
That it may make me patient, not irritable,
That it may make me broad in my forgiveness, not narrow,
haughty, and overbearing.
May no one be less good
for having come within my influence.
No one less pure, less true, less kind, less noble
for having been a fellow-traveler

in our journey toward eternal life.
As I go my rounds from one distraction to another,
let me whisper from time to time,
a word of love to Thee.
May my life be lived in the supernatural,
full of power for good,
and strong in its purpose of sanctity.

The second form of practice is tapas. The literal meaning of the word tapas is 'to burn'. The idea is that through practice the impurities in the mind are burned away. Yoga scholars refer to the practice of tapas in three ways. The first is as a discipline of voluntary relinquishment. It could be likened to the Catholic practice of penance during the Lenten season. This may take the form of sexual abstinence, giving up a particular craving or pleasure such as the consumption of chocolate or alcohol, or any number of things. This form of tapas is quite valuable because it clearly reveals the level of attachment we have to the object of our desires. Jesus said it this way to a young man, "'If you want to give it all you've got, go sell your possessions; give everything to the poor. All your wealth will then be in heaven. Then come follow me.' That was the last thing the young man expected to hear. And so, crestfallen, he walked away. He was holding on tight to a lot of things, and he couldn't bear to let go."[116]

Accepting suffering as a means of purification is the second way that tapas is practiced. "Blessed is the man who is patient under trial and stands up under temptation, for when he has stood the test and been approved, he will receive the victor's crown of life which God has promised to those who love Him."[117] Situations that challenge us to remain firm in our convictions and consistent in our behavior provide the greatest

42

opportunities for spiritual development and personal growth. When we view life from the Divine perspective instead of our limited ego-centered vision, we can actually rejoice in tribulation knowing that our perseverance will result in proven character.[118] The questions to ask ourselves during times of suffering are, "What is the lesson for me in this, and what responsibility do I have in this situation?" The challenge is to learn the lesson that turmoil provides without allowing ourselves to wallow in self-pity or fall into a mire of depression. "If God is for us, who can be against us?"[119] We can face each hardship with the knowledge that God is always with us and that through this trial, we can grow in wisdom and understanding that will affect how we move through the rest of our lives. The victory is in standing firm in our faith and keeping our minds stayed on God. When we look to the light, there is no darkness. And although during our time of challenge we may feel sadness, we know that we can move through our emotions to the peace that is on the other side. "After you have suffered for a little while, the God of all grace, who calls you to share His eternal glory in union with Christ, will Himself perfect you and give you firmness, strength, and a sure foundation."[120]

Self-discipline, or diligently choosing to follow our personal code of ethics, is the third form of tapas. Jesus said, "Do for others just what you want them to do for you."[121] When we live in an ethical way, we present ourselves "as a living sacrifice to God, dedicated to His service and pleasing to Him."[122] We are called to be holy in all that we do, just as God who called us is holy,[123] for "faith without actions is dead."[124]

Paul tells us to imitate God as well-beloved children.[125] It takes determination and discipline to follow this dictate. "Those who belong to Christ Jesus have crucified the flesh with its passions and desires. If we live by the Spirit, let us also walk by the

Spirit."[126] So how do we imitate God? We know that God is love,[127] and Paul gives us a clear picture of the nature of love in I Corinthians 13:4-8. Because we know that God is love, let's replace the word *love* with *God*:

God endures long and is patient and kind.

God never is envious, nor boils over with jealousy.

God is not boastful or vain, is not haughty.

God is not conceited or rude, does not act unbecomingly.

God does not insist on His own rights or His own way.

God is not self-seeking.

God is not touchy, fretful, or resentful.

God pays no attention to a suffered wrong.

God does not rejoice at injustice or unrighteousness.

God rejoices when right and truth prevail.

God bears up under anything and everything that comes.

God is ever ready to believe the best of every person.

God's hopes are fadeless under all circumstances.

God endures everything without weakening.

God never fails.

Armed with this knowledge, in every circumstance we ask the question, "What would God/Love do?" The answer is right before us when we refer to I Corinthians 13. In all of our behaviors, we can say, "Could I see Jesus doing this or acting this way?" To practice tapas as a Christian means to imitate Him and to follow His commandments with all earnestness. This self-discipline involves the tireless examination of every thought, word, and deed. It would seem to be an impossible task when we rely on our own strength, but we know that Christ lives within us[128] and that we can do all things through Him who strengthens us.[129] To the degree that we discipline our-

44

selves in this way, is the degree to which we experience peace of mind. Practice does not have to be perfect to bring favorable results. That is why it is called *practice* and not abiding in perfection! We simply do the best we can, pick ourselves up when we fall, and try again.

If we fail to follow the standards we have set for ourselves, it is imperative that we forgive ourselves and move on. "If we confess our sins to God, He will keep His promise and do what is right; He will forgive us our sins and purify us from all our wrongdoing."[130] Clinging to past mistakes will just begin a train of negative thinking that will increase our suffering and block the flow of abundance in our lives. Paul said, "The one thing I do, however, is to forget what is behind me and do my best to reach what is ahead."[131] He encouraged, "Let your hope keep you joyful, be patient in your troubles, and pray at all times."[132]

The Christian life is meant to be one of abundant joy. If you are walking in a state of unhappiness, you are missing out on all the goodness that God has planned for your life "Who richly and ceaselessly provides us with everything for our enjoyment."[133] Jesus said, "I came that they may have and enjoy life, and have it in abundance."[134] When we walk in love, we experience true and lasting happiness. All of us have experienced that when we dwell in anger, resentment, un-forgiveness, and hatred, we suffer. The solution is living a life of love. It is so simple and beautiful, but it takes discipline (tapas). The effort is well worth it, however, because when we intentionally live a life whose goal and purpose is to love, then the peace of God guards our hearts and minds *and* all things are given to us, even to overflowing.

Question of the Day: In what area of your life do you need more discipline?

Happy Thoughts to Remember

Be holy in all that you do, just as God Who called you is holy.[135]

For the time being no discipline brings joy, but seems grievous and painful; but afterwards it yields a peaceable fruit of righteousness to those who have been trained by it.[136]

The effect of righteousness will be peace, and the result of righteousness will be quietness and confident trust forever.[137]

---

116 Matthew 19:21-22
117 James 1:12
118 Romans 5:3-5
119 Romans 8:31
120 I Peter 5:10
121 Luke 6:31
122 Romans 12:1
123 I Peter 1:15
124 James 2:26
125 Ephesians 51
126 Galatians 5:24-25
127 I John 4:8
128 Colossians 1:27
129 Philippians 4:13
130 I John 1:9
131 Philippians 3:13
132 Romans 12:12
133 I Timothy 6:17
134 John 10:10
135 I Peter 1:15
136 Hebrew 12:11
137 Isaiah 32:17

Day 10: Study

This is true knowledge, to seek the Self as the true end of wisdom always. To seek anything else is ignorance.

Do you find yourself riding the rollercoaster of offense? You know, getting offended at every little remark someone makes, taking things personally, if so-and-so breathes funny it must be about me! Yeap, that's codependence at its finest. Our culture calls people like that "sensitive." Let me tell you, if you don't already know for yourself, that it is a miserable way to live! Maybe your gig is fear of losing face. Perhaps you take offense when someone "makes" you look bad. It certainly is a hard pill to swallow. The bottom line is that we can find many reasons to choose to become offended. Yes, you read it correctly. Offense is a choice. The good news is that we get off of the offense roller-coaster by becoming aware. And like everything else, awareness takes practice.

Study is the third form of practice. It involves two things: study of the self and study of sacred scripture. "He who gets wisdom loves his own soul; he who keeps understanding will find good."[138]

47

Study of the self refers to knowing what things prompt you to react with negative thinking and behavior. If you are acquainted with what your hot buttons are, then you are better equipped in situations where they get pushed. Awareness is the first step in breaking the cycle of undesirable behavior. As evangelist, Kate McVeigh, says, "Offense is a bait to trap you."[139] The key to handling offense effectively is in recognizing the bait. When you are unaware of what your triggers are, then you are constantly taking the bait and riding the roller-coaster of blame, anger, and/or sadness.

Other people's behavior is not about you. It is a reflection of *their* character. You have a choice in how you react to offensive speech and behavior, but first you must know what sets you off. Do you need to prove that you're right in all situations? That is a bait. Do you want to always look good or to be understood as nice? That is a bait. Are there specific speech patterns or behaviors performed by other people that "get your goat"? Don't give your power of self-determination away. And don't get caught up in judgment. Love pays no attention to a suffered wrong.[140] We're all human, which means we all make mistakes. Recognize the bait, take your eyes off of that person, and fix them intently on God/Love. "The Lord will keep in perfect peace him whose mind is stayed on Thee."[141] Then you may choose to say to yourself, "That's not about me. Father, forgive them they know not what they do." (Because truly they don't, and neither do you!) But first, you must know yourself.

The second type of study is immersion in sacred scripture. It is essential that we elevate our minds daily with the Word of God. Reading the bible feeds us with the spiritual nourishment that we need to be successful in our love walk. It fuels our passion for God and sets the mood for our day. Just as the body requires good quality food daily to keep it in working order, so too do our minds need to be built up with the highest thoughts. Study increases our knowledge of God and His will, reminds us of who we really are, increases our faith, and helps to maintain our focus on the things that will benefit us, rather than drag us down. What we spend time studying, what we immerse ourselves in, will be what we rely on for comfort and support in our daily lives. We must fill our minds so full of the Word of God that it becomes firmly rooted in our hearts. With this foundation, our thoughts and speech will naturally reflect what we have fed ourselves. An hour of watching a graphically violent movie lowers the vibration of the spirit into the evil of the world; but even five minutes of reading God's Word lifts us into the energy of Love. We can literally feel the difference of these two resulting effects in our bodies. When we plant the seeds of violence, lust, self-condemnation, and greed in our consciousness, those are the plants that will grow. When we sow seeds of love, kindness, generosity, and power into our inner gardens, our plants will grow to produce a positive and joyful harvest.

Set time aside each day to read your bible and uplifting literature. Choose favorite verses that encourage you and write them on index cards to read throughout the day. Continually remind yourself of your new nature in Christ and the mission that He has given you. The importance of constant study cannot be overemphasized. Without it, we draw from empty wells. We must build ourselves up daily, reading scripture, praying, and meditating, so that from our *overflow* we can serve others, thereby dwelling in happiness and glorifying God. "Whatever things are true, whatever things are honest, whatever things are just, whatever things are pure, whatever things are lovely, whatever things are of good report; if there be any virtue and if there be any praise, think on these things."[142]

Question of the Day: What offends you the most?

Happy Thoughts To Remember

We refute arguments, theories, and reasonings and every proud, lofty thing that sets itself up against the knowledge of God; and we lead every thought and purpose away captive into the obedience of Christ.[143]

Be well balanced, be vigilant and cautious at all times; for that enemy of yours, the devil, roams around like a lion roaring, seeking someone to seize upon and devour.[144]

Attend to my words; consent and submit to my sayings. Let them not depart from your sight; keep them in the center of your heart. For they are life to those who find them, healing and health to all their flesh.[145]

---

138 Proverbs 19:8
139 Mark 6:3
140 I Corinthians 13:5
141 Isaiah 26:3
142 Philippians 4:6-8
143 II Corinthians 10:5
144 I Peter 5:8
145 Proverbs 4:20-22

Day 11: Surrendering To God

Let it Be
by Paul McCartney

When I find myself in times of trouble,
Mother Mary comes to me speaking words of wisdom,
"Let it be." And in my hour of darkness,
she is standing right in front of me speaking words of wisdom,
"Let it be." Let it be, let it be, let it be, let it be.
Whisper words of wisdom, let it be.
And when the broken-hearted people living in the world agree,
there will be an answer, let it be. For though they may be parted,
there is still a chance that they will see.
There will be an answer, let it be.
Let it be, let it be, let it be, let it be.
There will be an answer, let it be.
And when the night is cloudy,
there is still a light that shines on me.
Shine until tomorrow, let it be.
I wake up to the sound of music.
Mother Mary comes to me speaking words of wisdom,
"Let it be." Let it be, let it be, let it be, let it be.
There will be an answer. Let it be.

I'm not the ruler of the cosmos, but sometimes it appears, by my behavior, that I think I am. There are actually times when I think that I'm in control. How freeing to know that I'm not God. It's not my job, not my responsibility. So why do I keep taking on the task? Oh, come on now, you know what I mean. We, as humans, try to manipulate things so that they come out the way we want them to. We try to control people. It's quite laughable when you stop to think about it. I mean really, who do we think we are? Yes, we create, but we're not the Creator! We've all heard the admonition, "Let go, and let God." It's a nice, lofty, spiritual phrase. But what does it mean in practice? It means that when you're tempted to fix people, you don't. When you want to open your mouth, you keep it shut. And you keep your focus on your job, which is simply to love; so that when you do something, anything, you do it without expectation of reward. It's no small task, but the one that leads to freedom.

The fourth form of practice is surrendering to God. Paul said, "Offer yourselves as a living sacrifice to God, dedicated to His service and pleasing to him."[146] What would a life lived completely for God look like? It would be faith-filled and unconditional. We have no control over the outcome of our actions or the behavior of other people; we just think we do. This is a great illusion. The only things that we truly have control over are our own thoughts, words, and behavior. When we open our tightly closed fists relinquishing the illusion of control, we have room to receive the blessings that God wants to pour into our open hands. Jesus told us not to worry about anything at all. He said that if we focus on God (Love), all things would be provided for us.[147]

Much of the time, even when we are acting out of our best intentions, we still have a motive of reward. When I'm doing something *for* someone, I expect a reward. It may be as small an affirmation as, "Thank you." It might be as big an expectation as thinking that now that person is indebted to me. Simply put, we are often attached to the outcomes of our behaviors. "If I act this way, then that must be the result." "If I treat this person like this, then they will do that for me." The truth is, however, that we have no control over the results of our actions. We can't cause circumstances to come out a certain way, and we can't determine the behavior of other people. We have enough dealing with just ourselves. Our thoughts, words, and actions are the only things under our control.

The idea of surrendering to God all of the outcomes of our actions is that we expect *nothing* in return. This concept applies not only to a specific act that we plan and execute, but also to our day-to-day dealings in the world. It applies to the workplace and to the home. For instance, when you are working, whom are you working to please? Paul put it this way, "Whatever may be your task, work at it heartily from the soul, as something done for the Lord and not for men, that you will receive the inheritance which is your real reward. The One Whom you are actually serving is the Lord Christ, the Messiah."[148] When we do everything for God, we know that He has already abundantly blessed us with His love and provision. For what more could we ask? His love and provision are the ultimate blessings. God will never let us down. When we do something expecting a certain outcome, we most certainly will be disappointed from time to time. Then the action is conditional. We are working for reward rather than as a love offering to our Creator.

For seven years I worked as a massage therapist. Many people came to me suffering from pain. When I worked on them, my goal was to be as loving and kind as I could be in the moment, to apply my knowledge, and to stay present with them. I could not be attached to the idea that I was successful if when I was finished, they were pain-free; or conversely, if they were still in pain, that I had failed. Can you see that my only failure would have been not to do my best? That best was to surrender the efforts of my work completely to God. The rest was out of my control.

53

Every moment of your life is an opportunity to serve God. When you pick up that piece of litter, you are serving God. When you mow the lawn or wash the dishes, you are serving God. When you speak patiently and kindly to that sassy teenager, you are revealing a heart of worship. Your life can be an offering of adoration or a collection of one self-centered act after another. The practice of surrender is accomplished one moment at a time.

With every breath we take, let us praise the Lord. With every thought we think, let us praise the Lord. With every word we speak, let us praise the Lord. With every deed we do, let us praise the Lord. Every day, in every way, let us surrender to God. Your will be done, Father. Your will be done. Let it be.

Question of the Day: In what areas of your life are you still trying to retain control?

Happy Thoughts to Remember

Your Father in heaven knows that you need all these things. Instead, be concerned above everything else with the Kingdom of God and with what he requires of you, and he will provide you with all these other things.[149]

Whatever you do, whether you eat or drink, do it all for God's glory.[150]

And we know that in all things God works for the good of those who love Him, who have been called according to His purpose.[151]

146 Romans 12:1
147 Matthew 6:31-33
148 Colossians 3:23-24
149 Matthew 6:31-33
150 I Corinthians 10:31
151 Romans 8:28

54

Day 12: The Eight Limbs of Yoga; Non-violence & Truthfulness

From *Being Peace*

By Thich Nhat Hanh

Without being peace, we cannot do anything for peace. If we cannot smile, we cannot help other people to smile. If we are not peaceful, then we cannot contribute to the peace movement.

Jesus said that we must be perfect as our heavenly Father is perfect.[152] Would you like to stop reading and give up right now? Yeah well, me, too, if I don't gain some perspective. The slogan, "Practice makes perfect," is true. We are being molded into the image of the Son of God, and molding takes time. We all know that we will not achieve perfection until our true nature in Christ is revealed, and we understand that we are forgiven as we forgive. The seeds of holiness that we plant every day are what bring us joy. What we sow, we reap. The joy is in the practice.

In the Yoga Sutras, Patanjali further expounds on the practice of yoga by delineating eight limbs or parts which encourage the building of discipline.[153] These practical suggestions are intended to assist us in cleansing our minds and cultivating wisdom. The eight limbs of yoga are the yamas (abstinences), the niyamas (observances), asana (posture), pranayama (breath control), pratyahara (sense withdrawal), dharana (concentration), dhyana (meditation), and samadhi (absorption in God).

The yamas and niyamas are a code of ethics set forth as the groundwork for the practice of yoga. There are five yamas or abstinences. They may be thought of as universal moral tenets. The first is non-violence. Jesus said, "Happy are those who work for peace; God will call them His children!"[154] The call to non-violence is a high calling, and it begins with keeping our eyes on God/Love. When we only see God, then even in the most trying of circumstances we are rooted in peace. Jesus taught that 'an eye for an eye' is out-dated. Rather, if someone strikes you on the one cheek, offer him the other in response.[155] Remember I Corinthians 13? Love endures long and is patient and kind. It bears up under anything and everything that comes. A person who is firmly rooted in non-violence radiates a peaceful presence that positively affects the space around him or her. That person is a light for the world.

So, how does non-violence play out in real world situations? It starts with recognizing Jesus in everyone we encounter. Jesus said that whenever we do something for the least of His brothers, we do it for Him.[156] Life provides many opportunities for us to be less than kind. Would we yell at that person if she were Jesus? Would we give her the cold shoulder? She *IS* Jesus in disguise. Sometimes Jesus is disguised as an angry, offensive person or maybe someone who cuts us off in traffic. Under the mask, it's still Jesus.

Non-violence also begins with seeing Jesus in yourself. Do you truly believe that Christ lives within you?[157] You have this one life and your body is the temple of the Holy Spirit.[158] You are violent with your physical self when you eat too much, drink too much, and sleep too little. You are violent with your mental and emotional selves when you refuse to forgive yourself and dwell on thoughts of self-condemnation. You deny your spiritual self the peace that passes understanding when you forget who you are. Jesus taught that you must love your neighbor *as you love yourself.*

The first yama of non-violence is the fertile soil for all the other yamas. We are drawn to peaceful people as ones in whose company there is hope and rest. When we come from a non-violent perspective, we make room for the seeds of compassion and other God-like qualities to grow.

The second yama is truthfulness. Death and life are in the power of the tongue. What we say can preserve life or destroy it. There is a consequence to our words.[159] Jesus taught that everyone will have to give account of the words that he has spoken. They will set us free or declare us guilty.[160] He also taught that if we believe in our hearts, we can have what we say.[161] We are made in the image and likeness of God. He spoke the world into existence.[162] There is power in the spoken word. "A good person brings good things out of his treasure of good things; a bad person brings bad things out of his treasure of bad things."[163] What we believe, we therefore speak.[164] "The one who guards his mouth preserves his life."[165]

Truthfulness is essential in our love walk. When we practice speaking only the truth, we keep our channels free and clear. We speak the truth, and we have nothing to hide. When there is dishonesty in our lives, we have a sense of discomfort and uneasiness, often accompanied by fear. Jesus said, "If you abide in my word, you are truly My disciples. And you will know the Truth, and the Truth will set you free."[166] The word of Jesus is love for God and each other. We must not only communicate the truth, but we must use love as our barometer in our speech. Is brutal honesty non-violent? The answer, of course, is no. So truthful speech must be tempered by love.

Just for today, choose to be peaceful. Just for today, choose to be honest. Just for today, live with integrity. Today is your day one choice at a time.

Question of the Day: In what ways are you violent with yourself?

Happy Thoughts to Remember

Love your enemies, do good to those who hate you, bless those who curse you, and pray for those who mistreat you.[167]

Do not lie to one another, for you have put off the old self with its habits and have put on the new self. This is the new being which God, its Creator is constantly renewing in His own image, in order to bring you to a full knowledge of Himself.[168]

A good man eats good from the fruit of his mouth.[169]

---

152 Matthew 5:48
153 Sutra 2:29
154 Matthew 5:9
155 Matthew 5:38-39
156 Matthew 25:40
157 Colossians 1:27
158 I Corinthians 6:19
159 Proverbs 18:20-21
160 Matthew 12:34-37
161 Mark 11:22-24
162 Genesis 1:3, Hebrews 11:3
163 Matthew 12:35
164 II Corinthians 4:13
165 Proverbs 13:3
166 John 8:31-32
167 Luke 6:27-29
168 Colossians 3:9-10
169 Proverbs 13:2

Day 13: Non-stealing, Non-hoarding, & Sexual Continence

Psalm 24:1, 23:1

The Earth is the Lord's and the fullness of it,
the world and they who dwell in it.
The Lord is my Shepherd, I shall not lack.

Are you like me? I've been keeping stuff at my home just in case I ever need it. You know the stuff that you don't even know is still lurking in the dark corners of your closet? I'm talking about that stuff. I haven't used some of these things in years! I've been keeping things "just in case." Well, I had a moment of enlightenment recently when I realized that I was blocking the flow of abundance into my life by keeping all this stuff that I don't use. I understood that I don't need to keep stuff just in case. God will provide what I need when I need it. What a freeing revelation! I started getting rid of stuff right and left. In fact, I'm still doing it. Why? Because I want to demonstrate my faith and open myself up to receive.

The next two yamas deal with our attitudes toward the material things in our lives. These yamas are non-stealing and non-hoarding. Truly nothing in our lives is our own, not even our bodies. When we die, everything that we consider as a possession in the present time will be left behind.

We cannot take anything with us. The material things that are with us, our bodies, and the people in our lives have been entrusted to our care, but we do not own them. Rather, we are stewards of everything in our lives, the precious gifts that God has bestowed. "Who, then, is the faithful and wise servant? He is the one that his master will put in charge, to run the household and give the other servants their share of the food at the proper time. How happy that servant is if his master finds him doing this when he comes home! Indeed, I tell you, the master will put that servant in charge of all his property."[170] It is up to us to decide what kind of care we will take of what has been given to us. The better care we take of what we have, the more and better will be given to us.

God has provided everything we need for an abundant and fulfilled life. Jesus said, "Give to others, and God will give to you. Indeed, you will receive a full measure, a generous helping, poured into your hands—all that you can hold. The measure you use for others is the one that God will use for you."[171] What we sow, we reap. Stealing and hoarding cannot produce abundance in our lives. In fact, these actions will ensure a state of lack, a closed door to the inflow of excellent provision. The love of money and possessions keeps us bound into a state of fear of loss. We remain grounded in our greed and attached to the idea of material wealth, instead of keeping our focus on God. As we remind ourselves that God is our source and allow things to flow freely into and out of our lives, we make room for ever increasing abundance. When we cling to things, we have no room for new and better. We must let go of the old to welcome in the new. We must walk with open hands to truly experience freedom.

Prosperity is a blessing as long as we can give it all away. What we seek, we will find.[172] If we seek wealth, we will find it, but we will not find God. As surely as we will have $365 dollars at the end of a year if we put one dollar in a box every day, so we will find God if we invest in Him. Jesus taught that if we seek God first, then all things will be given to us.[173] When we make loving and serving God our number one priority, then prosperity seeks us.

The final yama is sexual continence. "For the desires of the flesh are opposed to the Spirit, and the desires of the Spirit are opposed to the flesh. . . And those who belong to Christ Jesus have crucified the flesh with its passions, appetites, and desires. If we live by the Spirit, let us also walk by the Spirit."[174] Our human nature naturally seeks carnal pleasures, and God "richly and ceaselessly provides us with everything for our enjoyment."[175] When our natural desires are held within the boundaries of love, respect, and service, we experience joy. When we are self-centered and self-seeking, we will eventually reap the consequences of our selfish actions. "The mind of the flesh is death, but the mind of the Spirit is life and soul peace both now and forever."[176] God promises that the effect of righteousness will be peace.[177] But for the person who is not sexually continent, "His own iniquities shall ensnare the wicked man, and he shall be held with the cords of his sin. He will die for lack of discipline and instruction, and in the greatness of his folly he will go astray and be lost."[178] Jesus taught that if a man looks at a woman with lustful desire, then he has already committed adultery with her in his heart; that it would be better to pluck out his eye than to experience the resulting hell that an unfaithful life brings.[179] It all comes back to this one thing: to experience peace and joy in all areas of life, we must keep our eyes on God/Love.

If you are married, this relationship is your first ministry. Paul said, "Sexual drives are strong, but marriage is strong enough to contain them and provide for a balanced and fulfilling sexual life in a world of sexual disorder. The marriage bed must be a place of mutuality—the husband seeking to satisfy his wife, the wife seeking to satisfy her husband."[180] You are no longer two, but one flesh, joined by God.[181] It is not about what you can get out of it. It is about what you give to it. It is not about you and your needs, nor about your spouse. Marriage is a call to love and serve God by loving and serving your spouse. Being faithful to your spouse is also being faithful to God. The one who is faithful abounds with blessings.[182]

Just for today, choose to be generous. Just for today, ask, "How can I serve?" Right now choose to know that all is provided for you and that your job is to love.

Question of the Day: What have you been holding on to that you need to give away?

Happy Thoughts to Remember

The Lord your God will make you abundantly prosperous in every work of your hand, in the fruit of your body, of your cattle, of your land, for good.[183]

My God will liberally supply your every need according to His riches in glory in Christ Jesus.[184]

Set me like a seal upon your heart, like a seal upon your arm; for love is as strong as death, jealousy is as hard and cruel as Sheol. Its flashes are flashes of fire, a most vehement flame.

170 Luke 12:42-44
171 Luke 6:38
172 Matthew 7:8
173 Matthew 6:33
174 Galatians 5:17, 24-25
175 I Timothy 6:17
176 Romans 8:6
177 Isaiah 32:17
178 Proverbs 5:22-23
179 Matthew 5:28-29
180 I Corinthians 7:2-4
181 Matthew 9:16
182 Proverbs 28:20
183 Deuteronomy 30:9
184 Philippians 4:19

Day 14: Niyamas; Purity & Contentment

From *The Wizard of Oz*

By L. Frank Baum

Aunt Em had just come out of the house
to water the cabbages when she looked up
and saw Dorothy running toward her.
"My darling child!" she cried,
folding the little girl in her arms
and covering
her face with kisses;
"Where in the world did you come from?"
"From the Land of Oz," said Dorothy gravely.
"And here is Toto, too. And oh, Aunt Em!
I'm so glad to be at home again!"

I live in a small town. People have sometimes remarked to me, "I could never live in a small town. There's nothing to do." These are interesting statements to me because my life is very full of activity. Just like everyone else, I tend to shopping and household duties. On the recreation side, I play games with my family, read, attend church, participate in extracurricular activities, visit people, sit on my porch, and in general, enjoy my life. So the question arises, "What do you have *to do* to be content?" Why do we sometimes feel like we have to go somewhere, other than where we are, to be happy?

There are five niyamas or personal observances. The niyamas may be understood as instructions for character building and self-discipline. We have discussed the last three niyamas in-depth: discipline, study, and surrendering to God The first niyama is purity. Jesus promised that the pure in heart will see God.[185] The practice of purity involves monitoring what we take into and how we care for our bodies. "As the One Who called you is holy, you yourselves also (must) be holy in all your conduct and manner of living."[186] This includes carefully choosing what types of music to listen to, shows to watch, books to read, the state of our home environment, and personal hygiene from a healthy diet and exercise, to proper cleanliness. We are made in the likeness of God as spirit beings whose true nature is love and light. This God-imaged spirit is housed in our bodies. Paul says that with this in mind, we must honor God and bring glory to Him in our bodies.[187]

Sometimes we compromise our purity in favor of just a little bit of smut. It happens in almost all areas of our lives. We eat food that is not good for us, watch movies that have just some violence and sexual content, or make a so-called "benign" comment about the sex appeal of someone other than our spouse. It's harmless, right? Maybe, maybe not. Moderation in some areas is a desirable path. Ironically, though, we wouldn't consider drinking just a little bit of arsenic or loosening the brakes on our vehicle just a tad. How much compromise do you allow in your life? Jesus put it this way, "Make certain, then, that the light in you is not darkness. If your whole body is full of light with no part of it in darkness, it will be bright all over, as when a lamp shines on you with its brightness."[188]

The second niyama is contentment. This practice refers to consciously being aware of, grateful for, and pleased with what you have and the gift of each moment. Contentment lies within you. You cannot find it outside of yourself. We all know that the grass is not greener on the other side. Like Jon Kabot-Zinn observed, "Wherever you go, there you are." You cannot escape the reality of your inner world.

Any place that you inhabit can be heaven or hell. The choice is yours. Contentment is only a thought away. Jesus said that the kingdom of God lies within us[189] and that if we seek it first, all things would be added to us.[190] This inner kingdom is "righteousness, peace, and joy in the Holy Spirit."[191] The outer world provides only temporary pleasures. To truly be content, we must look within. The peace which surpasses all understanding is always there waiting for us.

Our own judgments about life can affect our experience of contentment. Many of us are caught in the habit of labeling every circumstance that comes our way as either good or bad. If an unmarried woman gets pregnant, we label it "bad." If we get a promotion, we call it "good." And on it goes. But truly circumstances are neither good nor bad. They just are. In fact, they just are opportunities to shine the light of Christ.

Our judgments about circumstances create accompanying emotions. To get off of the emotional rollercoaster, we must stop the judging. Jesus' advice, "Do not judge," results in contentment.[192] I like the way Edward Hays put it, "Let us be temples then, and not courthouses!"[193] If we truly believe that all things work together for good, then we can greet every circumstance with a sense of equanimity, knowing that it will ultimately work out for the good of all concerned.[194] In fact, we can go a step further and begin thanking God for the good that will come out of the circumstance.

Gratitude is the secret to contentment. When we count our blessings, we are immediately reminded of the goodness of life. We have been given this one life, this one day. If we see from an eternal God-perspective, then we know the preciousness of the moment. There is no room for complaining when we understand who we are and our mission as light-bearers. To live is Christ, and to die is to gain the glory of eternity.[195] It is when we forget our true nature that we suffer. Paul expressed it so eloquently when he said, "I've learned by now to be quite content whatever my circumstances. I'm just as happy with little as with much, with much as with little. I've found the recipe for being happy whether full or hungry, hands full or hands empty. Whatever I have, wherever I am, I can make it through anything in the One who makes me who I am."[196]

Just for today, choose to think pure thoughts. Just for today, choose to be content. Just for today, remember that now is all there is. If you are not happy here, then where? If you are not happy now, then when?

Question of the Day: What do you think you have to have in order to be happy?

Happy Thoughts to Remember

Make a decisive dedication of your bodies as a living sacrifice, holy and well pleasing to God, which is your reasonable service and spiritual worship.[197]

Delight yourself in the Lord and He will give you the desires of your heart.[198]

Do not be anxious about anything, but in everything, by prayer and petition, with thanksgiving, present your requests to God. And the peace of God, which transcends all understanding, will guard your hearts and your minds in Christ Jesus.[199]

---

185 Matthew 5:8
186 I Peter 1:15
187 I Corinthians 6:19-20
188 Luke 11:35-36
189 Luke 17:21
190 Matthew 6:33
191 Romans 14:17
192 Matthew 7:1
193 from *In Pursuit of the Great White Rabbit* by Edward Hays

194 Romans 8:28
195 Philippians 1:21
196 Philippians 4:11-13
197 Romans 12:1
198 Psalm 37:4
199 Philippians 4:6-7

67

Day 15: Asana, Pranayama, Pratyahara, Dharana, Dyana, & Samadhi

From *The Precious Present*
By Spencer Johnson, M.D.

My past was the present.
And my future will be the present.
The present moment is the only reality I ever experience.

One of my favorite times of the day is early in the morning when I sit down with my big cup of tea to read the bible and meditate. It feels so good to withdraw into my "prayer closet" with minimal external stimulation. I relish the quiet peace of the morning and the lovely view of the sky as the sun rises over the horizon. These times of stillness are so very important for my spiritual and mental renewal. They bring me back to the awareness of now, where my experience of the world is as an eternal moment—oneness.

The next six limbs of yoga deal with physical practice and its results. These are asana, pranayama (discussed earlier), pratyahara, dharana, dyana, and samadhi. Asana refers to posture or seat. Patanjali says only one thing in the yoga sutras about posture, that it should be steady and comfortable. This is where the practice of yoga as physical exercise comes in. The poses and movements of yoga were developed so that the yogis of old could sit comfortably to meditate. When we experience aches and pains in our bodies, it is much more difficult to keep the mind focused on anything other than those sensations. Additionally, as our bodies age, they become drier and stiffer. The physical practice of yoga helps to keep the muscles toned and flexible and the joints mobile and well-lubricated. Not only does the physical practice of yoga entail whole body movement, but also eye exercises and cleansing practices for the internal organs. Many excellent books have been written about keeping the body fit through physical yoga.[200]

Pratyahara is sensory withdrawal. In our western society, we are bombarded by all sorts of sensory input, from radio and television to cell phones and billboards. We have many distractions that have the potential to draw us away from the kingdom of God within us. Jesus empowered people. He told them that God loves them; they are a light for the world; and the kingdom of God is within them. We must stop looking outside and giving away our power.

"Jesus came into Galilee, preaching the good news of the kingdom of God and saying, the time is fulfilled, and the kingdom of God is at hand; repent and believe the good news."[201] Church leaders of Jesus' time, the Pharisees, were looking for a revolution to establish their concept of God's kingdom on Earth. So they asked him when this kingdom would be established. But Jesus said that they were missing the point. The good news is that the kingdom of God is within you.[202] This glorious kingdom is righteousness, peace, and joy in the Holy Spirit.[203]

Jesus repeatedly emphasized that to enter into this here and now state of being, one must become like a little child, trusting, lowly, loving, and forgiving.[204] Children laugh and cry easily. They receive gifts with eager gusto. They have no concept of resentment or bitterness. Children live in the moment with energy, enthusiasm, and the rapture of life's simple pleasures.

Jesus said that each one of us has the potential to grow in right-eousness, peace and joy. He likened this kingdom potential to a tiny seed or bit of leaven that when planted in our own garden or swelled in the oven of our consciousness, will grow to such heights as to provide nesting ground for others or food for their souls.[205] He said that our number one priority in life must be to seek this kingdom, and all things would be provided for us as well.[206]

All wisdom can be found by turning within and listening to the "still small voice."[207] It is essential to take the time to withdraw our atten-tion from the outer world and to focus on the center of our being where we are not influenced by what societal forces say we should or should not do or be. Jesus, our example, spent much time alone in prayer. [208] He taught us, "Go into your most private room and closing the door, pray to your Father, Who is in secret."[209] The seed of the kingdom within us grows when we water it with our attention. Paul said, "Do not be conformed to this world, fashioned after and adapted to its external, superficial customs, but be transformed by the renewal of your mind, so that you may prove *for yourselves* what is the good and acceptable, per-fect will of God, even the thing which is good, acceptable, and perfect in His sight for you."[210] We must look within. This is pratyahara.

Dharana or concentration is the precursor to meditation. It is concerted attention directed toward one object, be it a mantra, a sound, or an object. Dyana or meditation is the cessation of thought which leads to samadhi, abiding in the awareness of your union with Christ. Jesus calls to us saying, "Come to Me, all who are weary and heavy-laden, and I will give you rest. Take My yoke upon you, and learn from Me, for I am gentle and humble in heart; and you shall find rest for your souls."[211] Come to Me as a child. "Be still and know that I am God."[212]

Just for today, breathe out resistance and breathe in gratitude. Just for today, listen to the still small voice within you. Today and always, know that your bliss will only be found within.

Question of the Day: In what way do you need to detach yourself from outside influences?

Happy Thoughts to Remember

The Lord will keep in perfect peace him whose mind is stayed on Thee.[213]

A calm and undisturbed mind and heart are the life and health of the body, but envy, jealousy, and wrath are like rottenness of the bones.[214]

Let us throw off everything that hinders and the sin that so easily entangles, and let us run with perseverance the race marked out for us. Let us fix our eyes on Jesus, the author and perfecter of our faith, who for the joy set before him endured the cross, scorning its shame, and sat down at the right hand of the throne of God.[215]

---

200 See for instance, The Complete Illustrated Book of Yoga by Swami
        Vishnu-devananda
201 Mark 1:14-15
202 Luke 17:21
203 Romans 14:17
204 Luke 18:17, Matthew 18:3, Mark 10:15
205 Matthew 13:31-33, Luke 13:18-21
206 Matthew 6:33, Luke 12:31
207 I Kings 19:12
208 Luke 5:16, Luke 6:12, Luke 22:41, Matthew 26:39, Mark 14:35
209 Matthew 6:6
210 Romans 12:2
211 Matthew 11:28-29
212 Psalm 46:10
213 Isaiah 26:3
214 Proverbs 14:30
215 Hebrews 12:1-2

Day 16: Obstacles to Happiness: Ignorance of Who You Are

Look at the birds of the air; they neither sow nor reap
nor gather into barns, and yet your heavenly Father
keeps feeding them. Are you not worth much more than they?
And who of you by worrying and being anxious can add one unit
of measure to his stature or the span of his life?
And why should you be anxious about clothes?
Consider the lilies of the field and learn thoroughly how they
grow; they neither toil nor spin. Yet I tell you, even Solomon in all
his magnificence was not arrayed like one of these.
But if God so clothes the grass of the field,
which today is alive and green and tomorrow is tossed
into the furnace, will He not much more surely clothe you,
O you of little faith?

I am God's beloved. I am God's most cherished creation. I am God's chosen one. How about you? I hope that you are at a point in your life where you know, like me, that nothing can separate you from the love of your Father.

Jesus came to seek and to save that which was lost.[216] He came so that we might have and enjoy life in abundance.[217] He came to call us to repentance and to teach us to love.[218] Jesus came to tell us who we are.

Those of us who are lost are walking around with bags over our heads. We don't know who we are. We're caught up in our own little worlds, without consideration of a larger purpose for life or the welfare of people outside our circles. We view life as suffering, so we might as well accept it. We identify with our bodies. When it goes, we go. So we take as much as we can because we may not be here to get anything tomorrow.

Jesus came to tell us that we're missing the point. He taught that if we repent, then life has meaning and fulfillment. The word *repentance* means to change your mind. It is the stepping out of the ego-self and into God reality. It is a call to stop seeing yourself as a limited human being and to start seeing yourself as God sees you. He taught us to open our eyes, "You are a light for the world!"[219]

There are five obstacles to happiness, living that enjoyable life of abundance that Jesus demonstrated.[220] The first is ignorance of who we are. Without an understanding of who we really are, our lives lack meaning and purpose; we are externally motivated, our happiness dependent upon circumstances. But the glorious truth is that, "It's in Christ that we find out who we are and what we are living for. Long before we first heard of Christ and got our hopes up, God had his eye on us, had designs on us for glorious living, part of the overall purpose He is working out in everything and everyone."[221]

The bible teaches us that we are made in the image and likeness of God,[222] that we are His very own children.[223] To understand our true nature, then, it is essential to know what God is like. The bible is very clear on the nature of God. God is Spirit.[224] God is Love.[225] God is Light, and there is no darkness in Him at all.[226] This means, then, that being made in the image of God that *we* are spirit beings whose true nature is love and

73

light. Wow! What a concept! This knowledge puts a whole new twist on life. We are not just human animals destined only to eat, sleep, and get as much pleasure as we can before we bleep off of the planet. We are not just these bodies. We are eternal. And with this eternal nature comes a divine plan. Jesus said, "You have not chosen Me, but I have chosen you, and I have appointed you that you might go and bear fruit and keep on bearing, and that your fruit may be lasting."[227] We are spirits on a mission.

The bible also teaches us that we have been foreordained, justified, and glorified.[228] Our Creator has called us by name[229] and justified us through the sacrificial life of our Saviour.[230] God knows our names. He knows our thoughts.[231] He knew us before we were born.[232] He knows everything about us. He created us and called His creation good! We are God's beloved, His chosen instruments for good works,[233] welfare, and peace.[234] We are heirs of the promises that say that all the works of our hands are blessed; that we are the head and not the tail, that we are blessed coming in and going out; that our Father delights in prospering us.[235] We matter to God and are important in His divine plan. We, as the children of our omnipotent Creator, are being transformed into the image of Christ from one degree of glory to another![236] Is it beginning to sink in for you that you are precious in His sight and He loves you?[237] You matter. And more than that, your destiny is to be molded into the image of Christ.[238] Paul said it this way, "Do you not yourselves realize and know thoroughly by an ever-increasing experience that Jesus Christ is in you?"[239]

We are spirits on a mission to tell the world that God exists; God loves us; God desires eternal fellowship with us; we are made in His image, to love and be loved, and that the way to the knowledge of God is through Jesus. Think of all the people that you know personally who are without purpose and fulfillment in their lives. They don't know who they are. They don't know that they have been called, chosen, and are precious to their Father. They don't know that they mat-

74

ter. That is why our mission is so important. We are God's voice to call them home. We are God's arms to embrace them. We are God's eyes to see them when they think that no one notices. We are Christ's ambassadors.[240] We are the manifestation of His love today.

So here's how it plays out. When you go to the grocery store, your goal may be to buy food, but your mission is to be a light to the checkout clerk. When you go to the doctor, your goal may be to get medicine for what ails you, but your mission is to be a light to the doctor and staff. When you go to work, your goal may be to complete your assigned tasks, but your mission is to be a light to everyone you interact with. At home, your goal may be to be the best spouse, parent, or roommate that you can be, but your mission is to be a light to everyone you live with.

Trust in who God says you are. Choose to believe. Now we see dimly as in a mirror, but one day we will be in the presence of our Father, and we will know. We will know. The absolute truth of who we are in Christ will be revealed to us, and in that moment we will comprehend that God is Love, and we are love. God is Light, and we are light. God is Spirit, and we are spirit. Jesus came to find us and bring us back into the knowledge of God. He was the Light manifested, Love personified. He called us and gave us our mission. And this is what he said, "You are a light for the world."[241]

Question of the Day: Do you define yourself as, "What I will be when I grow up," or "Who am I being now?"

Happy Thoughts to Remember

I am made in the image and likeness of God. (Genesis 1:27)
God is Light, and I am light. (I John 1:5)
God is Love, and I am love. (I John 4:16)
God is Spirit, and I am spirit. (John 4:24)
I am God's beloved. (John 3:16)

I am God's very own child. (I John 3:1)
I am precious to God, and He loves me! (Isaiah 43:4)
I am called according to God's purpose. (Ephesians 1:11)
I am foreordained, justified, and glorified. (Romans 8:30)
I am more than a conqueror through Christ who loves me.
(Romans 8:37)
I have the mind of Christ and hold the thoughts of His heart.
(I Corinthians 2:16)
I am a fellow heir with Christ. (Romans 8:17)
I am God's own chosen one, purified, holy, and well-beloved.
(Colossians 3:12)
I am God's own handiwork, recreated in Christ Jesus.
(Ephesians 2:10)
I am a new creature in Christ. The old has gone, and the new has come.
(II Corinthians 5:17)
I am the righteousness of God in Christ. (Philippians 3:9)
I am an over-comer because He Who lives in me is greater than he
who is in the world. (I John 4:4)
I am a light for the world. (Matthew 5:14)

---

216 Luke 19:10
217 John 10:10
218 Matthew 18:3, John 13:34
219 Matthew 5:14
220 Sutra 2:3
221 Ephesians 1:11
222 Genesis 1:27
223 I John 3:1
224 John 4:24
225 I John 4:16
226 I John 1:5
227 John 15:16
228 Romans 8:29-30

229 Isaiah 43:1
230 Acts 13:39.
231 Psalm 139:2
232 Psalm 139:16
233 Ephesians 2:10
234 Jeremiah 29:11
235 Deuteronomy 28; Deuteronomy 30:9
236 II Corinthians 3:18
237 Isaiah 43:4
238 Romans 8:29
239 II Corinthians 13:5
240 II Corinthians 5:20
241 Matthew 5:14

Day 17: Egoism

John 13:12-17

"Do you understand what I have done to you?
You call Me the Teacher and the Lord,
and you are right in doing so, for that is what I am.
If I then, your Lord and Teacher, have washed your feet,
you ought to wash one another's feet.
For I have given you this as an example,
so that you should do what I have done to you.
I assure you, most solemnly I tell you,
a servant is not greater than his master,
and no one who is sent is superior to the one who sent him.
If you know these things, blessed, happy,
and to be envied are you if you practice them."

Pride is a very difficult thing to deal with because it often masks itself as justified resentment. But, you see, I've come to understand that there is no justified resentment. I think that many times when I feel bitter or resentful, it is because my pride is involved. I don't want to lose face. As Christians, we are called to the high road, the one that "bears patiently with suffering which results when you do right and that is undeserved."[242] The calling also includes readily adjusting ourselves to people, never overestimating ourselves, being humble and long-suffering.[243] "Love does not insist on it's own rights or it's own way, for it is not self-seeking."[244] That's big, because my flesh is defensive and likes to prove my point in all situations. But I have also experienced the unfathomable peace that comes from keeping my mouth shut and suffering in silence. That is when I look more like Jesus and less like me.

The second obstacle to happiness is egoism, putting self before God. It may be likened to following a mirror that we're holding in front of us. All we see is ourselves, the kingdom of me. But we will not have one moment's peace by thinking about ourselves first. We just think we will. To get ourselves out of the way and put Love first can be a scary thing. We make ourselves vulnerable and open to rejection. We become afraid. Yet, when our actions are motivated by personal gain, with no consideration for others, we suffer. "That's what happens when you fill your barn with self and not with God."[245]

Selfishness, personal interest, and the desire to get our own way lead to dissatisfaction, rather than contentment. Lasting happiness will not be found by always putting ourselves first; "I, me, mine! I, me, mine! What about me?!" "If your first concern is to look after yourself, you'll never find yourself. But if you forget about yourself and look to Me, you'll find both yourself and Me."[246] The great paradox is that it is in the letting go of self that we gain everything. When we are so stuck on getting our own needs met, we lose out on the blessings that come from giving and serving others. Jesus said that there is more happiness in giving than receiving.[247] Dwelling on ourselves, our desires, our problems, and our pains will never lead to joy. It is only when we step out of ourselves and our little worlds and place our focus on God and His unconditional love, that we find true peace. Jesus said, "Who of you by worrying and being anxious can add one unit of measure to his stature or to the span of his life? . . . Instead, be concerned above everything else with the Kingdom of God and with what He requires of you, and He will provide you with all these other things."[248]

Many of our relationship conflicts, problems at work, and areas of discontent may be linked to our own self-centeredness. Things didn't go our way, and we dwell on it. The other person said something that stung our ego, and we lash back. We must prove that we're right at all costs. This way will never lead to happiness.

So, the next time you are suffering, ask yourself, "How am I putting myself first?" You may be surprised at the insight you receive. Happiness is only a thought away, but it is your choice. Are you willing to let go and get yourself off of your mind? "The Lord will keep in perfect peace him whose mind is stayed on Thee."[249]

Question of the Day: In what areas of your life have you let your pride get in the way of peace?

Happy Thoughts to Remember

If anyone would come after me, he must deny himself and take up his cross and follow me. For whoever wants to save his life will lose it, but whoever loses his life for me will find it.[250]

Whoever wants to be first must place himself last of all and be the servant of all.[251]

Happy are the humble, who rate themselves insignificant, for theirs is the kingdom of heaven![252]

242 I Peter 2:20
243 Romans 12:16; Matthew 5:3, 5
244 I Corinthians 13:5
245 Luke 12:21
246 Matthew 10:39
247 Acts 20:35
248 Matthew 6:27-33
249 Isaiah 26:3
250 Matthew 16:24-25
251 Mark 9:35
252 Matthew 5:3

Day 18: Idolatry

Psalm 34

I will extol the Lord at all times;
His praise will always be on my lips.
My soul will boast in the Lord; let the afflicted hear and rejoice.
Glorify the Lord with me; let us exalt His name together.
I sought the Lord, and He answered me;
He delivered me from all my fears.
Those who look to Him are radiant;
their faces are never covered with shame.
This poor man called, and the Lord heard him;
He saved him out of all his troubles.
The angel of the Lord encamps around those who fear Him,
and He delivers them.
Taste and see that the Lord is good;
blessed is the man who takes refuge in Him.
Fear the Lord, you His saints,
for those who fear Him lack nothing.
The lions may grow weak and hungry,
but those who seek the Lord lack no good thing.
Come, my children, listen to me;
I will teach you the fear of the Lord.

Whoever of you loves life and desires to see many good days,
keep your tongue from evil and your lips from speaking lies.
Turn from evil and do good; seek peace and pursue it.
The eyes of the Lord are on the righteous
and His ears are attentive to their cry.
The face of the Lord is against those who do evil,
to cut off the memory of them from the earth.
The righteous cry out, and the Lord hears them;
He delivers them from all their troubles.
The Lord is close to the brokenhearted
and saves those who are crushed in spirit.
A righteous man may have many troubles,
but the Lord delivers him from them all.
He protects all his bones, not one of them will be broken.
Evil will slay the wicked;
the foes of the righteous will be condemned.
The Lord redeems his servants;
no one will be condemned who takes refuge in Him.

My friend, Anjanette, tells the story of the day that she woke up to the fact that she had made her boss at work into an idol. She didn't like him. She didn't want to spend all of her time with him. She didn't sigh with longing whenever he walked into the room. No, that was far from the case. Rather, she obsessed about him and all of the ways that he "made" her life miserable. Anything that gets that much attention has become an idol. The key to her transformation was taking her eyes off of him and putting them on God.

Idolatry is the third obstacle to happiness. God is our source for everything. He is our source for love, peace, prosperity, health, and happiness. Idolatry is putting other things, people, or situations before God. There are two types of idols: attachments and aversions. Attachment idols are your strong preferences. What do you look for

81

as your source of peace, joy, and happiness? For instance, do you look to your spouse as your ultimate source for unconditional love, praise, and affection? What a burden that is for any one person to bear! Your spouse is God's gift to you. Imagine that you are a wife. The task before you then, is to love and care for your husband as the precious gift that he is. Your husband is not designed to meet all of your needs for love. He can only shine his particular beauty. To expect anything more is unrealistic. This understanding can free you up to appreciate your husband for the gift that he is, to care for him better, and to release the burden of expectations that he cannot possibly meet. After all, he is not God, is he? He is not your source.

Do you look to food to find happiness? You may enjoy the taste and texture and experience a sense of fullness, but you will be hungry again; and again, and again, and again. Food cannot satisfy you completely. Do you look to the mall to fill a sense of void within you? Shopping can bring a temporary high, but once the item is on your table or in your closet, the newness wears off and the need reappears. Do you turn to alcohol or other drugs to get high? Once the drugs are metabolized out of your system, your search will begin again. Do you seek perfect, unconditional love in your relationships? Some days people will meet our needs and other days they won't. Do things have to be or happen a certain way for you to be happy? Paul said, "Shun any sort of idolatry, of loving or venerating anything more than God."[253]

Aversion idols are your pet peeves, anything that "gets your goat." Aversion is a form of idolatry because it has your attention. Anything that takes your eyes off of God in an obsessive way is an idol. Do you obsess over politics? Does being around smokers "drive you mad"? Is there a family member that you just "can't stand"? What problem seems insurmountable? What or whom do you allow to steal your peace? This is your aversion, and holding on to anger about this or that will never bring you peace. Paul's advice rings true, "If possible, as far as it depends on you, live at peace with everyone. . . Do not let

82

yourself be overcome by evil, but overcome evil with good."[254]

What is your idol? Making an idol of something or someone is often an unconscious process. Once you have identified your idol(s), then you have the awareness and power to change. We suffer when we seek fulfillment from finite wells. The answer is always to look to God as our Source. His love and provision will never run out. "Seek your happiness in the Lord, and He will give you your heart's desire. Give yourself to the Lord; trust in Him, and He will help you; He will make your righteousness shine like the noonday sun."[255]

Question of the Day: What has become an idol in your life?

Happy Thoughts to Remember

Let Almighty God be your gold, and let Him be your silver, piled high for you. Then you will always trust in God and find that He is the source of your joy.[256]

You shall have no other gods before me. You shall not make for yourself an idol in the form of anything in heaven above or on the earth beneath or in the waters below. You shall not bow down to them or worship them.[257]

Seek first His kingdom and His righteousness, and all these things shall be added to you.[258]

---

253 I Corinthians 10:14
254 Romans 12:18-21
255 Psalm 37:4-6
256 Job 22:25-26
257 Exodus 20:4-5
258 Matthew 6:33

Day 19: Fear of Death

Romans 8:31-39

*If God is for us, who can be against us? He who did not spare
His own Son, but gave Him up for us all—how will He not also,
along with Him, graciously give us all things?
Who will bring any charge against those whom God has chosen?
It is God who justifies. Who is he that condemns?
Christ Jesus, who died—more than that, who was raised to life—
is at the right hand of God and is also interceding for us.
Who shall separate us from the love of Christ?
Shall trouble or hardship or persecution or famine
or nakedness or danger or sword? As it is written:
"For your sake we face death all day long; we are considered as
sheep to be slaughtered." No, in all these things we are more
than conquerors through Him who loved us. For I am convinced
that neither death nor life, neither angels nor demons, neither the
present nor the future, nor any powers, neither height nor depth, nor
anything else in all creation, will be able to separate us from the
love of God that is in Christ Jesus our Lord.*

The final obstacle to happiness is fear of death or clinging to
life. We are God's most cherished creation, His beloved. When we

lack this confidence, however, we cling to life and identify the body as who we are. The cosmetics and beauty industries tell us that we must look like twenty-five year old people until we die. We are practically encouraged to view aging as an unnatural part of the life cycle, something to be avoided because certainly it will lead to reduction in physical beauty and ultimately death. Well, of course, beauty is not only in the eye of the beholder, but a product of a loving spirit. "Let not yours be the merely external adorning with elaborate interweaving and knotting of the hair, the wearing of jewelry, or changes of clothes; but let it be the inward adorning and beauty of the hidden person of the heart, with the incorruptible and unfading charm of a gentle and peaceful spirit, which is very precious in the sight of God."[259] And our bodies do eventually die. But if we trust in our true nature, we know that the essence of who we are in Christ lives on. Jesus has "completely set free all those who through the haunting fear of death were held in bondage through the whole course of their lives."[260] It all comes back to faith.

Children take the attributes of their parents. They are made in their image. We, too, are made in the image of our Creator. We are spirits who were created as love and light. God loves us completely, intimately, and unconditionally. When we truly have a deep understanding of this concept, we need never feel lonely or forsaken. We are loved and highly valued! The authority of our Creator has been bestowed upon us. We must assume our role as God's beloved children, showing our true nature by loving each other and living fearlessly. "There is no fear in love; perfect love casts out all fear."[261] Because we know that God is Love, we can understand it this way, "There is no fear in *God*; *knowledge of God* drives out all fear!"

Jesus promised, "For God so greatly loved and dearly prized the world that He gave up His only begotten Son, so that whoever believes in Him shall not perish but have eternal life."[262] In this knowledge, there is no fear. Jesus said that eternal life is knowing God and

Himself.[263]   He said that what God wants is for us to believe.[264] That's it, straight and simple.   "If you acknowledge and confess with your lips that Jesus is Lord and in your heart believe that God raised Him from the dead, you will be saved. For with the heart a person believes and so is justified and with the mouth he confesses and confirms his salvation."[265] God does not require us to be a certain way or do a certain deed to please Him. "For it is by free grace that you are saved through faith. And this is not of yourselves, but it is the gift of God; not because of works, lest any man should boast."[266] He only wants us to seek Him and to follow Jesus.

Eternal life, yoga, is now. When we put ourselves aside and accept the righteousness of Christ, we experience God-reality. To be "in Christ" means to be in Love. Jesus said, "I give you a new commandment: that you should love one another. Just as I have loved you, so you too should love one another. By this shall all men know that you are My disciples, if you love one another."[267] We have complete confidence now and after physical death because we know that we know that we know that Jesus is the Light manifested and Love personified; and we have awakened to the fact that we are of Him. This knowledge is manifested in our love. "We know that we have passed over out of death into Life by the fact that we love the brethren." [268]

There is no fear in love. To overcome fear of death, we must have faith in God. Jesus said, "Do not let your hearts be troubled. You believe in and rely on God; believe in and rely also on Me. In My Father's house there are many dwelling places. If it were not so, I would have told you; for I am going away to prepare a place for you. And when I go and make ready a place for you, I will come back again and will take you to Myself, that where I am you may be also. And where I am going, you know the way."[269] The way is faith manifested by love. "For in Christ Jesus, neither circumcision nor uncircumcision counts for anything, but only faith activated, energized, expressed and working through love."[270] "Be determined and confident. Do not be afraid. It is the Lord your God Who is with you. He will not fail nor abandon you."[271] For, "There is nothing in all creation that will ever be able to separate us from the love of God which is ours through Christ Jesus our Lord."[272]

Question of the Day: In what ways have you allowed fear to hold you back?

Happy Thoughts to Remember

Peace I leave with you; My own peace I now give and bequeath to you. Not as the world gives do I give to you. Do not let your hearts be troubled, neither let them be afraid. (Stop allowing yourselves to be agitated and disturbed; and do not permit yourselves to be fearful, intimidated, cowardly, and unsettled.)[273]

For God did not give us a spirit of fear, but of power, love, a calm and well-balanced mind, discipline, and self-control.[274]

I have told you these things, so that in Me you may have peace and confidence. In the world you have tribulation, trials, distress, and frustration; but be of good cheer! For I have overcome the world. (I have deprived it of power to harm you and have conquered it for you.)[275]

---

259 I Peter 3:3-4
261 I John 4:18
263 John 17:3
265 Romans 10:9-10
267 John 13:34-35
269 John 14:1-4
271 Deuteronomy 31:6
273 John 14:27, Amplified Bible
275 John 16:33, Amplified Bible

260 Hebrews 2:15
262 John 3:16
264 John 6:29
266 Ephesians 2:8-9
268 I John 3:14
270 Galatians 5:6
272 Romans 8:39
274 II Timothy 1:7

Day 20: Putting It All Together: Christian Yoga & The Way of Happiness

Colossians 3:12-14

Therefore, as God's chosen people, holy and dearly loved,
clothe yourselves with compassion, kindness,
humility, gentleness, and patience.
Bear with each other and forgive whatever grievances
you may have against one another.
Forgive as the Lord forgave you.
And over all these virtues put on love,
which binds them all together in perfect unity.

The practice of Christian yoga is being the simple presence of Love; it is rebirthing into eternal life which is knowledge of God and Jesus. In eternal life, we find happiness. There are five obstacles to happiness: ignorance of who you are, egoism, attachment, aversion, and fear of death. These obstacles may be overcome through four practices: effort toward steadiness of mind, discipline, study (of self and the bible), and surrendering to God. The practice of discipline involves the five things Jesus taught: love, forgiveness, authority, using your talents, and sowing and reaping.

Jesus' example of living was a roadmap to happiness. He sacrificed his life, secure in the knowledge of Who He was, leaving behind His own will, attachments, aversions, and fear. He even went so far as to give us a discourse on happiness.[276] It goes like this:

If you want to be happy . . .

1. Be humble and rate yourself insignificant.
2. Know that it is an opportunity when you have lost what is most dear to you. Then you will seek your comfort in God and have the revelation of His matchless grace.
3. Be meek, mild, patient, and long-suffering.
4. Hunger and thirst for righteousness and communion with God.
5. Be merciful.
6. Be pure in heart.
7. Be a peacemaker and a maintainer of peace. Plant seeds of peace wherever you go.
8. Do what is right even when it is hard.
9. Speak the truth about Me (Jesus) and God's love for us even when it is not "cool."

And the rewards for such a life are incredible . . .

1. Yours is the kingdom of heaven.
2. You will be comforted by your relationship with God.
3. The world is yours.
4. You will obtain mercy.
6. You will see God.
7. You will take your place, fulfill your role as God's very own child.

So, "Today, if you will hear His voice, do not harden your hearts."[277] Happiness is only a thought away. What is your excuse? Are you still holding on to a view of yourself as a limited, purposeless being, or can you accept God's idea of you? Are you focused on getting your own way, or can you let go and let God? What do you think you *have* to have to be happy and what thing do you think *has* to change? Can you release your fear and have faith? Is your life just too stressful, your body too painful, your world too crowded to walk in love? The only thing standing in-between you and your bliss is **YOU**!

Question of the Day: What is one change you need to make today?

Happy Thoughts to Remember

Above all things, have intense and unfailing love for one another, for love covers a multitude of sins.[278]

For the whole law is compiled within the one precept: You shall love your neighbor as yourself.[279]

For this is the message which you have heard from the first, that we should love one another.[280]

---

276 Matthew 5:1-12
277 Hebrews 3:7-8
278 I Peter 4:8
279 Galatians 5:14
280 I John 3:11

Day 21: And So It Begins!

John 15:9-12

I have loved you just as the Father has loved Me;
abide in my love.
If you keep My commandments,
you will abide in My love and live on in it,
just as I have obeyed My Father's commandments
and live on in His love.
I have told you these things that My joy
and delight may be in you,
and that your joy and gladness may be of full measure,
complete, and overflowing.
This is My commandment: that you love one another
just as I have loved you.

God loves you completely and unconditionally. His marvelous plan involves you fulfilling your destiny as a light-bearer in such a way as to bring you supreme joy. You are absolutely unique. There is no one exactly like you in the whole world. You are not called to be someone else or to live someone else's life. You are called to be the best you that you can be. Your God-given talents were designed to bring you joy in the service of others. "For we are

God's own handiwork, recreated in Christ Jesus, that we may do those good works which God predestined for us, that we should walk in them, living the good life which He prearranged and made ready for us to live."[281] This knowledge is all we need to be truly content.

Much of our lives is wasted in traveling from one place to another, either physically or in our minds. We are always preparing for the next event, planning what we are going to do, anticipating a future activity. Hurry up and get there; hurry and finish; move over; get out of the way; hurry, hurry, hurry! When we live in the future, we lose our present joy and our sense of contentment knowing that God is providing absolutely everything we need in every moment. To feel "the peace of God which surpasses all understanding,"[282] we have to stop and be aware in the present moment. Our blessings are already here. We just keep missing them because we live in the future. "Let me hurry and finish the dishes so I can rest." "Let me get this grass cut so I can relax." This hurry-up-and-get-there attitude robs us of our awareness of our total provision in the present moment. Life happens in the blink of an eye anyway. We have to truly stop and experience the moment before it passes us by.

Look around you. Everywhere it is evident that God loves you. He provides you with outstanding sensual stimulation. Look at the trees how majestic they are, the face of a child, how bright. See the variety of colors that surround you. We are encompassed in a visual feast if we will but open our eyes. Listen to the sound of the wind chimes on a breeze, soothing music, the voice of a loved one. It is enchanting! The tastes and textures of the food we eat are practically endless. The hug of a friend warms our heart. These are the experiences that let us know that we are infinitely loved.

Everything in our lives is a gift from God. Your body is a gift. Your spouse is a gift. Your friends and children are gifts. Your home is a gift. Your clothes are a gift. The food you eat is a gift.

Do you see that these things are God's provision for your welfare and happiness? All you need do is to look, and you will see the gifts. "Yes, we should make the most of what God gives, both the bounty and the capacity to enjoy it, accepting what's given and delighting in the work. It's God's gift! God deals out joy in the present, the now."283

You have this one day. What will you do with it? How will you live? Live today as if this is your last opportunity to love. Love everyone you come into contact with. Truly be with them. Give them your attention. Love them as if they are the only person on the planet and you have all the time in the world! Enjoy everything you do today. Take pleasure in all the sights, sounds, smells, and tastes. Have fun! Do something you love to do. Walk in gratitude. "Behold, what I have seen to be good and fitting is for one to eat and drink, and to find enjoyment in all the labor in which he labors under the sun all the days which God gives him—for this is his part."284

Remember: You're on a mission, and you've been given this one day to complete it. Love as much as you can. Live out loud!

Question of the Day: What is one way that you can be a light in your world today?

Happy Thoughts to Remember

You have not chosen Me, but I have chosen you and I have appointed you, that you might go and bear fruit and keep on bearing; and that your fruit may be lasting, so that whatever you ask the Father in My Name, he may give it to you.285

The Spirit of the Lord God is upon me, because the Lord has anointed and qualified me to preach the Gospel of good tidings to the meek, the poor, and afflicted; He has sent me to bind up and heal the brokenhearted, to proclaim liberty to the captives and the opening of the prison and of the eyes to those who are bound.[286]

Go then and make disciples of all the nations, baptizing them into the name of the Father and of the Son and of the Holy Spirit, teaching them to observe everything that I have commanded you; and behold, I am with you all the days, to the close and consummation of the age.[287]

281 Ephesians 2:10
282 Philippians 4:7
283 Ecclesiastes 5:19-20
284 Ecclesiastes 5:18
285 John 15:16
286 Isaiah 62:1
287 Matthew 28:19-20

Appendix: Bible Affirmations

This is the day the Lord has made. I will rejoice and be glad in it. *Psalm 118:24*

The Lord is my Strength and my Shield. *Psalm 28:7*

God is my Refuge and Strength. *Psalm 46:1*

The Lord is my Shepherd; I have everything I need. *Psalm 23:1*

The Lord is my Light and my Salvation; I fear no one. *Psalm 27:1*

I can do all things through Christ Who strengthens me. *Philippians 4:13*

The peace of God guards my heart and mind in Christ Jesus. *Philippians 4:7*

I am more than a conqueror through Him Who loves me. *Romans 8:37*

Greater is He Who lives in me than he who is in the world. *I John 4:4*

God restores health to me and heals my wounds. *Jeremiah 30:17*

By His wounds I have been healed. *I Peter 2:24*

The Lord forgives all my sins and heals all my diseases. *Psalm 103:3*

The Lord surrounds me with goodwill, pleasure, and favor. *Psalm 5:12*

God supplies all my needs through His riches in Christ Jesus. *Philippians 4:19*

God's angels have charge over me to guard me in all my ways. *Psalm 91:11*

All the work of my hands is blessed. *Deuteronomy 30:9*

All things are possible to him who believes. *Mark 9:23*

All things are possible with God. *Matthew 19:26*

All things work together for good for those who love God and are called according to His purpose. *Romans 8:28*

I walk by faith and not by sight. *II Corinthians 5:7*

I am a light for the world. *Matthew 5:14*

Acknowledgements

Thank you, my Jesus, for giving me back my life.

Thank you Mom, A, Zack, and Joshua for being awesome in every way.

Thank you very much to my editor and dear friend, Athena duPre', who labeled the book, "magnificent," thereby planting the seed of hopeful expectation in my heart.

Thank you to all of my yoga students who faithfully attended classes every week and showed up at the retreats every year. You know who you are-I love you!

Thank you to all my teachers, especially Rev. Tommy Jackson, Sharon Gannon, David Life, Pastors Carl and Belinda Benton, and Rev. Brian Hotaling for your examples of humility, compassion, and kindness.

Thank you to Dottie Griffin and Anjanette Hebert for your unfailing love and support.

And a special thank you to my dear friends and "Rayne" yoga students, Paulette Leger, Beth Goins, Sylvia Peltier, Sheila Faulk, Andree' Wingate, and Connie Nini, who were with me week after week, year after year, every step of the way. You have my heart.

To Order Copies of

Jesus, Yoga, and the Way of Happiness

A Christian Yoga Daily Devotional

by **Andrea J. Vidrine**

I.S.B.N. 1-59879-181-8

Order Online at:
www.authorstobelievein.com

By Phone Toll Free at:
1-877-843-1007